Solo Acoustic Musician™

4

The Open Mic

Michael Nichols

Printed in the United States of America

Paperback ISBN: 978-1-961624-20-7
eBook ISBN: 978-1-961624-21-4

Canoe Tree
Press

Canoe Tree Press is a division of DartFrog Books
https://dartfrogbooks.com

TABLE OF CONTENTS

Definition of a Solo Acoustic Musician 5
A Solo Acoustic Musician's Code of Conduct 7
Introduction..9
Personal Updates..13
Open Mic vs. Open Jam 21
Songwriters in the Round 31
Check It Out First..39
Etiquette..47
Types of Listening...59
Networking 69
Hosting an Open Mic...77
Promoting the Open Mic...89
Find A Local Sponsor..97
Going Undercover..103
    Pesky Pelican...105
    North End Taphouse 125
    Brewers Tasting Room...141
    McArthurs Irish Pub 147
    Kahuna's 153
    All 5 Elements..159
    Ozona Brewing Company 163
    The Chill Room 169
    Micky Quinn's...175
    The Haus Coffee Shop & Wine Bar 181
    Snooty's Social House 189
    Crooked Thumb Brewery..193

Nolan's Pub 201
Chicago Jaqx Pizzeria and Taphouse 207
Creative Grape...211
Ragnar Race Vacation 215
Coast Guard Buccaneers..................................... 223
Afterword 229
About the Author.. 235
Acknowledgements..237

DEFINITION OF A SOLO ACOUSTIC MUSICIAN

Solo: Done by one person alone; unaccompanied.

Acoustic: Relating to sound or the sense of hearing. When referring to popular music or musical instruments: not employing electrical amplification.

Musician: A person who plays a musical instrument, especially as a profession, or is musically talented.

My definition of a Solo Acoustic Musician (SAM in the pages that follow) is straightforward: one person with an acoustic instrument, performing songs with or without vocals, hopefully for an audience.

There is something intrinsically pure about a person making music and singing songs with an acoustic instrument. To me, that's what a Solo Acoustic Musician is, and it's one of the most original forms of musical expression.

A SOLO ACOUSTIC MUSICIAN'S
CODE OF CONDUCT

Always be on time.

Dress appropriately for the gig.

Don't get drunk onstage or in the venue.

Clean up after yourself at the end of your gig.

Promote your music and your gigs.

Network with other musicians.

Use your gifts and talents to help others.

Show respect to yourself and others by not engaging in lewd language on the microphone.

Represent yourself, the agents, and the clients as best you can by being professional on the gig.

 **INTRODUCTION**

Here we are at the beginning of *Solo Acoustic Musician 4: The Open Mic,* and I am pretty excited to be writing about this topic.

Some of you may wonder why I have chosen to write a book about the open mic, and how it ties into the Solo Acoustic Musician series. Well, it all began when another SAM friend suggested that I think about the open mic as a topic for the series. I immediately realized that the idea made a lot of sense, because many Solo Acoustic Musicians take part in open mic night events at every level of their careers. Personally, I have gone to open mics to play my songs and I have been an open mic host as well. I have also supported open mics in the past simply by attending and being a patron of the venue. I like listening to the other SAMs play their songs, and spending a little money on food and drink. When I am busy gigging all the time and have a night off, sometimes it is fun to be an audience member.

As a beginner Solo Acoustic Musician, an open mic night event can be someone's first time getting on stage and performing in front of an audience. I know from experience that many SAMs have gotten their start by attending and performing at open mic events.

Making friends and networking with the other Solo Acoustic Musicians is a big part of the open mic night. These events often develop a local community, who attend regularly and get to know one another. A vital support system can grow in this environment. The open mic can lead to gigs and in many ways, it can be an audition.

Having an outlet to share and perform your original songs is another component of the open mic night event. Solo Acoustic Musicians who play songs at open mics are not doing it for the money; they are there to share the music and their passion. I have seen many different levels and blends of local SAMs congregating to enjoy a musical fellowship of sorts. Sometimes you can have a beginner SAM on stage, who is followed by a Solo Acoustic Musician with ten or twenty years of gigging experience. In general, everyone claps and shows support for each other while enjoying the music and learning about each other's lives through the songs and stories that are shared on stage.

As a full-time working Solo Acoustic Musician, I spend most of my time performing covers of other people's material. The open mic is a great creative outlet for SAMs like me who want or need a place to play their original songs. Open mic night events usually foster an environment that encourages musicians to share their personal stories and original songs on the stage. Quite a few of the open mics I have been to in the past have been geared especially toward the original music performer.

Having an appreciative audience for original material is an awesome thing. I have bought quite a few CDs from local musicians, and I discovered a lot of these people and heard their original music at open mics. I have also known many full-time Solo Acoustic Musicians who have done the same thing as I did in the past by attending open mic night events regularly. In a way, it's a rite of passage and also becomes a comfort zone for SAMs.

I have always felt relaxed and at home in the open mic environment. There is something about walking into a room full of people who have something in common. Playing guitar and singing is a common bond with almost everyone in the room at an open mic. Anyone attending an open mic who isn't there to play or join the list is probably a supporter of live music and is there to be supportive of all the performers.

As a host of an open mic night event, it can be a very cool experience to build and become a part of the community of musicians. It gives you a unique perspective, and it is important to be a host for other musicians. Providing a venue and running the sound while managing the list is a skill that can be developed into a way to fill a day of the week on the calendar. Being there every week as the host also means you will get to hear all of the music being shared.

In the Networking With Other Musicians chapter of SAM 1, I wrote briefly about hosting an open mic. I think this book will be quite an expansion from those two pages. In this book, I will discuss more about the networking topic as well as related issues like etiquette. I will talk about hosting an open mic and share my own experiences. Promoting an open mic night and finding a local sponsor will also be part of what I share with you. I have "gone undercover" and visited some open mics, taking notes so I can report to you what I saw and heard. I am excited to explore this topic in this way and share how it went and what I found.

Parts of the open mic experience are serious, but I think the overall atmosphere should be relaxed and all about Solo Acoustic Musicians having fun. I believe the open mic is an important part of the SAM lifestyle and I am excited to share my experiences.

 # PERSONAL UPDATES

In the past, I have had a year of time between these personal updates, but this time I was moving fast into SAM 4 and I was busy upgrading and replacing all kinds of gear. My iPad battery started to fail and was even struggling to hold a charge when plugged into the charger. I spent about two hundred dollars at the repair shop on a new battery and some faster better chargers. (Always buy two.) But in the end, after five years of service, my trusty iPad was failing, so I looked at buying a brand new one.

In hindsight, I could have saved a few bucks and gone with my instinct to buy a new one in the first place. I bought the same model I had before, but in the newest generation. When I got home and set it up, I wanted to insert it into to my protective case, but it didn't fit so I had to go back to the store. All in all, I went back and forth between the repair shop and the store about a dozen times during this process. The end result was a new 12.9 iPad Pro and a new protective case that fit my AirTurn Manos Universal Tablet Mount.

I looked at less expensive tablets to try and save some money. The iPad I bought is the biggest and most expensive model. I see it as an investment in my lifestyle (and a tax write-off) and I know that it will last for at least five years and probably more now that I have learned how to maintain my battery life in a better way.

I use the original Onsong app for my songbook and when I bought it, I paid a one-time lifetime fee. Now they charge the same amount for monthly access to the app. I looked at other apps, but I didn't see anything that I thought was comparable. Sometimes I don't like change, and change can be tough for anyone. I am used to keeping my songbook in the Onsong app and I wanted to stick with it for the future. Onsong is also only available on Apple products, so my hands were tied if I wanted to stay with the same app.

After I got everything set up and was logged in with my Apple ID, the app downloaded to my new iPad and my song-book was intact. I didn't have to transfer or import files or anything. I was so happy that it was just that easy, and I was able to go right back to work after a month of struggling with getting it all together.

I have a Gator brand pro backpack guitar case. I bought the biggest version they make — it's built to hold an acoustic guitar in the front and an electric in the back. I use the back compartment for my extra string binder, books and other merchandise like CDs and stickers, and my iPad mic stand clip.

I have had it for more than five years and I have made many repairs to it. I have had to break out the sewing kit to work on busted zipper tracks and sew busted handles back to the body of the case. One of the zipper pull tabs came off so I used a zip tie and a metal ring to create my own pull tab for it. The backpack straps have busted loopholes that I repaired, and there are holes in the inner lining of two of its compartments.

I use my gear a lot as a gigging Solo Acoustic Musician, so I put things to the test and they get a lot of wear and tear. Well, I decided to upgrade and downsize. I bought the pro model for one acoustic guitar, which is lighter and smaller. Since it's brand new, all the zippers work great and all the compartments are intact; I am happy I pulled the trigger on the purchase.

When I was emptying out the old case I was surprised at how much stuff I had in the inner pockets and extra storage compartments. I cleaned out unnecessary things and moved a few things that I need but don't use often to the extra gearbox in my van. Problem solved. A little sidenote for you is that Gator's headquarters are here in Tampa where I live but they don't manufacture or make repairs here. Yes, that did bum me out a little, but they are still one of the best and I love my new case.

The cart that I use to transport my gear from the house to the van and during load-ins and load-outs had a busted wheel that I rigged with a screw and some duct tape. I was in gear-updating mode and bought a new cart. I ordered it online and it turned out to be a little bit bigger than my old one, which is great, because it is even easier to move my gear around now.

Well, it didn't take long for a hole to rip in the lining. I broke out some Velcro and my sewing kit to create a patch on the inside of the cart. The hole was along the side, between the wall and the base, so using the Velcro kept it flexible and added strength. The cart folds up and the patch is working great. I have subsequently added zip ties for greater sustainability.

At the same time, the screws to the plastic anchors that attach the lining to the upper corners of the cart were falling out. Three of them are gone so far. I should probably just remove the last one because it is inevitable that it will loosen and be gone at some point. I fixed one with a shoelace, and another with twine, and the third was repaired with a zip tie.

The cart cost more than $100, so I plan to fix it as much as I can before I give in and buy a new one. By the way, I have added zip ties to my gearbox in the van along with the old standby of duct tape. I always used zip ties on my pedal board, and they can come in handy for a quick fix in many situations.

In January, I took my guitar to the shop for some love. It had been two years since I had been to see the luthier for a complete setup and I was in need of a neck adjustment and some overall care. I was tucking little pieces of business cards under my high E string to help with some fret buzz. I put them under the string on both the nut and the saddle. It takes a little maneuvering to get this right, but it can get you through until you can get to the luthier. Before I knew it, I was back for a new input. I have had my Martin for more than fifteen years and have had the input replaced before. I paid the premium price for the same Fishman brand model, and it's been working great ever since.

The travel case for my pedal board was in need of repair as well. The zipper — I swear I am hard on zippers — wasn't staying zipped. The track was opening after it was closed. I would just pull it to the middle and that was it. One spot holding the case closed while the rest of the track was wide open. I went to the repair shop and it would be more than a hundred dollars to fix so I went on the Pedaltrain website and ordered a new case. It's pretty sweet, and the zipper works. It also has a big side pocket that holds my extra string binder and the cables that I use to run the extra speaker I use on some gigs.

Have you ever debated with yourself about buying a product, or paying a little more for a lifetime, two-year, or five-year warranty? I purchased a DR Pro Tripod mic stand with a telescoping boom extension. The telescoping boom is one that has two adjustable sections instead of the solid one-piece boom on other stands.

The DR brand has offered different warranties over the years, and I kept my receipt, so when something breaks, I take it right back to the store where I bought it and they replace it immediately. I am on my eighth mic stand! It is an expensive model — around eighty dollars — and I keep my purchase receipt in the glove box of my van. It is one of the best purchases I have ever made, and I will probably buy another one someday. The current warranty is for two years; I think they changed it over time because of how many they were replacing.

Like I said, I have been updating gear like crazy and at a fast pace. I was using an octave pedal to help me create bass guitar parts in my loops. I purchased an Electro-Harmonix Bass9 and it has been well worth the money. I have it set on the precision bass guitar setting and worked out my levels for a great tone. It is a great addition to my pedal board.

I also took my Mackie Thump speakers that I have had for about five years to the store to trade in. It does seem like I'm in a five-year cycle. I am interested in looking at battery-powered options, and I made a decision while making sure I had Bluetooth capability. I traded up for two brand-new EV ZLX-12BT 12-inch speakers. It is awesome to be able to turn on music from my phone or my iPad or even my laptop if I want to do that. I got good value for my old speakers and spent a little cash for the balance but I am super happy. I did a lot of online research before going to three different stores just to see what was available.

I made a major change to my tip can sign after learning about landing pages. I went with the Linktree service for mine; they created a QR code and a URL for me to use and I can adjust my list of sites at any time. I have it set up to direct people to my Venmo, Paypal, and my music website, book website, merchandise store, and even my iTunes page. It is a really cool option for quick access, and people are becoming more accustomed to giving code scan tips.

I had two QR codes on my previous sign. One linked to my website and the other to my iTunes page. People would come up, scan one, and walk away. They weren't reading the sign and I wasn't getting those people's tips. I did have Venmo and Paypal written out on my sign, but some people don't read and just scan, so I noticed what was happening and made a change. It worked!

The codes remove a level of resistance. People can scan them from across the room, which is great because sometimes they don't want to walk up to me and tip. They also make it easy for people who don't have cash on them, which opens up their generosity. Making it as easy as I can for people to tip me is a good move.

I have booked a date with the same videographer I worked with on my last promo video. He has moved to Tennessee but is going to be in Florida in October. I am very excited to work with him again and make a new video. I believe it has been almost three years exactly, and he told me he has improved his skills and equipment, and has some new ideas for me, so I am looking forward to the experience. My video gets me a lot of work, so if I make an even better one I know it will be well received by venue representatives.

My life as a Solo Acoustic Musician is always evolving and that means I need to update things from time to time. I like all my new equipment updates and I look forward to updating my promo video as well as anything else I can that will improve my life as a SAM.

That can also mean updating and adjusting how I do things. You know that piece of paper and pen I told you that I keep in my pocket? Well, before I start my show or when I go on a break now, I spend a good five minutes walking around the room stopping at as many tables as I can and asking the people to tell me the name of a few bands that they like. I write them down quickly and move to the next table to do it again. I will start my next set playing songs by those bands, and it really does work for engaging the audience members and making tip money.

I used to wait for someone to make a request and always had my paper and pen to write down song titles, but this way is more forward and direct. I can also do it from the stage. I pull out my paper and pen and work my way around the room asking several or all of the tables for a band name. I write them down and set my notes on my side table where I can see it. It's fun and breaks the ice between me and the audience. If you haven't been doing it, give it a try.

 # OPEN MIC VS. OPEN JAM

There is a difference between an open mic and an open jam, although they are often referred to as if they are the same thing. When I think of an open mic night, I think of a Solo Acoustic Musician as being the host of the event. The host most likely provides their own PA and sets up the sound system, mics and stands.

The lineup of musicians could be solo, duo, or trio performers who play songs in an intimate setting. Most likely they would be using acoustic guitars, keyboards, banjos, mandolins, electric or stand-up bass, and percussion instruments like cajons, djembes, and bongos, plus the occasional tambourine or egg shaker.

Although playing cover songs is totally ok, most of these acoustic-style open mics focus on songwriters sharing their original compositions. They will typically be labeled as such, with a title like "singer-songwriter open mic night" or "original music showcase." Some will even have a featured performer for the evening, who gets to play a longer set of original music.

On the other hand, when I think of an open jam event, I usually imagine a full band as the hosts and providers of PA, along with a backline of amps and a drum set. The host band will typically start and end the jam with a short set of songs. A lot of open jams in my area are based on the blues, and that's probably because it can be easy to accommodate lots of different musicians who have never played together before. Picking a key and starting a pattern can be an easy way for everyone to get involved in making music together. Each lineup of musicians will probably get to try out three jams and then another group will get their turn. A typical host band would consist of two electric guitars, bass, and drums. The addition of a keyboard player and a horn, like a saxophone or a trumpet, could also be an extension of the core four-piece.

Let's look at some textbook definitions and information I found in my research. Even beyond my own understanding of these two events, there is a clear difference.

What's the meaning of an open mic? An event in which amateurs may perform usually without auditioning first.

An open mic (shortened from "open microphone") is a live show at a venue such as a coffeehouse, nightclub, comedy club, or pub, usually taking place at night, in which audience members may perform on stage whether they are amateurs or professionals, often for the first time or to promote an upcoming performance. As the name suggests, performers are usually provided with a microphone plugged into a PA system so that they can be heard by the audience.

Performers sign up in advance for a time slot with the host, who is typically an experienced performer or the venue's manager or owner. The host may screen potential candidates for suitability for the venue and give them a time slot to perform during the show. Open mics are focused on performance arts like comedy (whether it be sketch or stand-up), music (often acoustic singer-songwriters), poetry, and spoken word. It is less common for groups such as rock bands or comedy troupes to perform, mostly because of the space and logistical requirements of preparing and sound-checking such groups.

Open mics may have very low entrance fees or no entrance fees at all, although the venue itself may prepare a gratuity jar, a "pass the hat" for donations, or a raffle with various prizes.

Venues that charge no fees profit from selling alcohol and food. The performers are not typically paid, although the venue may give them a drink or a meal. If the host is an experienced professional and not the owner/manager of the venue, they are usually paid for their services and may perform at some point during the evening, either preparing a full performance of their own or filling in at short notice when a performer is unavailable. Open mics are somewhat related to jam sessions, in that they both see amateur performers being given the opportunity to perform. The difference is that jam sessions often involve musical ensembles, possibly even a house band or rhythm section, and may involve the participation of professional performers.

Although there are open mics that cater to comedians, spoken word poets, and rappers, we are focused on musicians, and here is some more information I would like to share with you in that context.

Open mics provide an opportunity for musicians to gain experience performing in front of a live audience without having to go through the process of getting traditional gigs, which is very difficult to do without experience or a demo recording. They provide an outlet for singer-songwriters.

Open mic events are most commonly held in the middle of the week. They are rarely held on Friday and Saturday nights, when venues are busy with weekend customers and most live music performances are probably played by professionals who have been booked.

A popular open mic arrangement is the "Blues Night." In this format, a bar or club will dedicate a particular night, usually in the middle of the week, as being "open mic blues night." The establishment may supply a house band, typically guitar, bass, and drums, and sometimes a keyboard. Singers, guitarists, and harmonica performers who wish to play sign up. The host is tasked with screening the performers, choosing and ordering, and getting the performers on and off stage in a polite manner.

Since the songs chosen need to be simple enough so that a band of musicians who have not played together can perform them without practice, blues standards are used. Songs might be announced as a "12-bar fast shuffle in C," or "slow 12-bar blues in F," or similar descriptions that should be familiar to all concerned. Lead singers, keyboards, horn players (usually saxophones or trumpets), and various percussion instruments are common additions.

Unlike the term "open mic," when I looked up the term "open jam" there was no specific definition. The term "jam session" was there in its place. I have heard both terms used and found the information to be accurate.

What does open jam mean? Open jam nights are usually held at bars. They are also held on weeknights, to get more people in the place. Musicians will fill the place up and drink, and suddenly Tuesday won't be an "off" night for the bar. Remember that playing in a jam situation is different than playing with friends in your garage.

A jam session is a relatively informal musical event where musicians, typically instrumentalists, play improvised solos and vamp over tunes, songs, and chord progressions. To "jam" is to improvise music without extensive preparation or pre-defined arrangements, except for when the group is playing well-known covers of existing popular songs. A jam can be used as a social gathering and practice session. Jam sessions may be based upon existing songs or forms, may be loosely based on an agreed chord progression or chart suggested by one participant, or may be wholly improvisational. Jam sessions can range from very loose gatherings of amateurs to evenings where a jam session coordinator or host acts as a "gatekeeper" so that appropriate-level performers take the stage together.

Years ago, I used to host open mic nights, and I will talk about that throughout this book but right now I want to share a very relevant story with you. I was hosting a singer-songwriter style open mic in a restaurant with a bar that also had a weekly blues jam on another weeknight. This venue was developing a reputation for having good blues music on the weekends. They were attracting high-caliber players for their blues jam night and it was becoming well known around the area. My open mic also always had at least fifteen musicians on the list.

One night when I was hosting, a couple arrived and the woman had a horn case with her. The man approached me and asked where the drum kit was. I said, "We don't have one."

He replied, "Well, I am here for the jam," and pulled a pair of drumsticks from his back pocket. He added that his wife had brought her saxophone and that they had come to "jam" with other musicians. I informed him that this was not that kind of event and asked him how he had heard about our gathering.

He said that they were visiting from out of town and he had seen the flyer hanging on the board at the local music store. I knew that I had labeled my open mic night as a singer-songwriter style event, both online and on the flyers. I kindly explained to him what we were doing and that the blues jam type of event that they would probably enjoy takes place on another night of the week.

I turned him over to the bartender and manager so he could get the details for the open jam. This is a great example of knowing the difference between an open mic and an open jam. I was explicit in my description of the event I was hosting and yet someone still misinterpreted the message on my flyer. I was grateful to know that people were seeing my flyers at the music stores, and happy that someone came to the venue, even if it was for the wrong reason. I am sure they came back for the open jam, and that only added to my working relationship with the venue.

Near my home is a town with a vibrant downtown area, and one of the most popular places has three completely different parts: a restaurant, a bar and lounge, and a nightclub. A local Solo Acoustic Musician I knew had started a Tuesday night open mic night back in 2011 and was telling all the other local musicians to come out and play their original songs. He was set up in the nightclub which to my mind was an interesting choice, as the venue and owners had what I thought would be much more appropriate atmospheres for an acoustic open mic night.

When I arrived after playing my own gig down the street, I went to find the host and sign up to play. He was happy to see me, I signed up, and I waited to play. At some point, a guy who played djembe and another guy who played bass came over to ask me if I wanted them to join me and play along with me on my songs. I politely declined and explained I was playing my original songs. Then the host came over and asked me on those guys' behalf and kind of tried to coax me into playing with them.

I repeated what I had already told them. I wasn't interested in "jamming out" on my original songs, and I wanted to perform by myself. When I got on stage, I played my first two songs, the crowd responded, and things were going well. About halfway through my third song, the bass player and djembe player started to play along with me.

The song I was playing was a soft ballad that I finger-picked, and it has a simple pattern of moving bass notes along with stationary high notes. When I finished the song the bass player said, "Hey, why did you stop the jam, man?" I replied that the song was three minutes and six seconds long exactly and it was not a jam. I also told him that I tune down half a step to E flat and although he thought he was watching my hands and duplicating my low-end bass line, he was in fact playing the wrong notes because he was tuned in standard. I continued by telling him I had politely said no to them playing along with me and then they just did it anyway which is very unprofessional. I added that on top of stepping all over my slow, soft ballad, he was playing the wrong notes and evidently couldn't even tell how bad it sounded.

My experience at that open mic started out going well and ended on a literally sour note. I never went back to that open mic, because as I told the host, he should have intervened and stopped them when they started playing along with me. The bass player was plugged into the PA system and not using an amp so the host could have easily turned the bass volume down from the mixer. It was a lesson learned, and I used it to be a better host myself.

I have gone to an open jam hosted by a band and asked to play my three songs for ten minutes by myself. The host band told me it was a jam and not a Solo Acoustic Musician open mic. They seemed to totally get the idea of it being a different kind of event.

Back around 2005, I was living in Baltimore and was toying around with putting a band together. A bass player and a drummer I knew were jamming out with me at home and we decided to go to an open jam that was hosted by a four-piece band every Tuesday night in Columbia, MD, which is between Baltimore and Washington D.C. The place had a great drink special, the host band was really good, and the place was packed every Tuesday night. We would not have to bring too much gear because the host band was providing the back line of amps and a drum set. My drummer friend brought his own snare drum, my bass player friend brought his bass, and I brought my guitar.

This story is just to show that sometimes a SAM does get to play their songs at an open jam, because every week this one guy who was about twenty-two years old would be there with his acoustic guitar. He only played Dave Matthews songs and he wasn't very good, but everyone clapped and cheered him on. One person even said he was the little train that thought he could. We befriended him and he told us all how he was trying to get good enough to go out and book his own gigs someday. He was driven and he kept coming back every week, so everyone accepted him into the fold. Sometimes I wonder if he ever did finally start getting his own gigs and playing music for a living. I can't think of any other time that I have been to an open jam where they let a SAM on the stage to play by themselves.

As a Solo Acoustic Musician, I am more inclined to go to open mic nights and perform. I consider open jams to be an electric guitar player's domain, and since I do not play electric guitar, I do not join in the jams. It wouldn't be impossible to plug in an acoustic-electric guitar and jam out, but it is not what I am into. It can be fun for me to go to an open jam and watch and listen to the good players making music together, though.

My personal preference in the open mic niche is the singer-songwriter style open mic night. It is the type of event that I have become most accustomed to over time, and it is what I really enjoy being a part of when I can get to one. Best of all is the original music singer-songwriter showcase with a featured artist performing a thirty-minute set of their own songs in a listening room environment. In my mind that is the pinnacle of the Solo Acoustic Musician open mic event.

What is a listening room? Listening rooms are similar to house concerts in that they are small venues that provide an intimate listening experience. But unlike house concerts, listening rooms are for-profit entities.

In my experience, listening rooms provide a small stage, a house PA system, mics, and stands. The venue will be focused on the performance like it is a private concert. To me, the term listening room implies that people will not be talking or watching a game on TV, but will be watching the performing musician and listening to their music. An audience of one hundred or fewer people all intently listening to Solo Acoustic Musicians sharing their original songs and stories is what I have experienced. This kind of open mic event attracts all levels of musicians, and there is a lot of shared respect among the people in the room. The listening room environment is completely music-focused, and that is hard to find in venues where the other customers are paying attention to and reacting to other things like sports on TV.

I hope that this information helps you understand the differences between open mics and open jams. If you have never had the experience of going to a listening room, then I hope you can find one and go. It is a wonderful and enlightening thing for a Solo Acoustic Musician.

 # SONGWRITERS IN THE ROUND

Close your eyes and imagine four of your favorite artists or singer-songwriters sitting on stools on a stage. Now imagine you are in the front row and are going to get to see and hear them play your favorite songs that they wrote. Add to that the possibility of them telling stories about the songs and the life experiences that inspired the lyrics and the feeling involved in creating the music. All four of them will take turns, playing one song at a time and then passing the invisible baton to the person next to them. It will be like a slow songwriters' relay race, around and around until they have all played several songs each.

Although this is not an open mic night event, it is in my opinion similar and also a part of the same niche for Solo Acoustic Musicians. I have even seen a songwriter round take place at an open mic night. Four SAMs decided to take the stage at the same time and share their songs separately. It can work if they are the next four musicians on the list and if they each play three songs total; that way, it will take the same amount of time as getting on the stage separately. A songwriter's round could also work as a featured artist slot to end an open mic night.

The similarities in these types of events are that there are several different musicians, often Solo Acoustic Musicians, who get to take turns sharing their songs. Open mic nights can have a list of SAMs signed up and can even have featured performers. A songwriter's round is like a three, four, or five-person featured artist performance. Some open mic events even do an online pre-sign-up for the list during the week before the actual date. The featured slot or in-the-round event is very similar, and planned ahead before the event.

A very important etiquette lesson for performing in a songwriter's round is being present in the moment. If you are on stage in a group, taking turns playing your songs in the round, then you have to be quiet and sit still when it is not your turn to play. Try not to do anything to distract the audience from the person who is performing their song. Do not check your phone or even turn it on while you are waiting.

Believe it or not, it can be hard to sit still for three to five minutes while someone plays a song. Mulutiply that by three or four times before you get to play your song, and then repeat the process a few times. A little meditative breathing and some active listening can help you pay attention to the other performers. It can be a challenge to stay engaged while sitting still and not fidgeting, keeping your attention on the performer.

---

*I love playing songwriter round events. The songs,
the creativity, and the chance to co-write with
other songwriters, means so much to me.*
—Kevin Mahoney, Knoxville, TN

I took part in a songwriter round back around 2012 at a multi-award-winning house concert venue in Tampa called The Yard. The venue is located at a residential house, and it has a lot of amenities. They have a covered stage that can accommodate a full band. The stage has walls and lights. The whole backyard has been turned into a live music venue that even includes a covered seating area. They have built a bunkhouse for traveling musicians who need a place to stay. They have built a bathroom building. On the back of the house is a covered screen porch where they put out tables for food and drinks.

Everyone is encouraged to bring a covered dish to share. The nearest hotel has been contacted and gives a discount to the people who travel in from out of town for a show at The Yard. I have probably left something out in my description, but I can assure you that they haven't missed a thing when it comes to making their venue great. They take care of the musicians and the fans who attend the concerts. The audience members are encouraged to bring a donation of fifteen to twenty dollars and one hundred percent of the money goes to the musicians.

I was invited by a friend to take part in a show at The Yard where there would be three performing artists. Steve and Jayne are musicians and have been friends of mine since I first moved to Florida. Steve invited me to join them in the show and I accepted his invitation. He explained the concept of sitting next to each other on stage and taking turns playing original songs. Jayne and I played solo, while Steve brought along the bass player from his band and they performed as a duo. Steve provided the PA system and we each had a bar stool to sit on. If I remember correctly this is the only time I have ever taken part in a songwriter round. I was excited to hang out with my friends and also to hear their music. As a full-time working Solo Acoustic Musician, I don't get the chance to do either of those things all that often.

I like being truthful with you, the reader, and I had brought along a half pint of scotch to put in my hot tea or coffee. I thought it might come in handy on such a cold day. Little did I know that the other musicians had done the same thing with different types of booze. We were all staying warm and rosy-cheeked that day. I don't make a habit of drinking on my gigs and I am totally against doing it now, but back then was a different time in my life and also it was a special kind of show and day in its own way. For some reason, we were all a bit comfortable having a nip of something to keep us warm and glowing.

At the end of the show, we all sold a bunch of CDs and people also threw tip money in our tip can. If I remember correctly, I sold sixteen CDs that day at ten dollars each. After everything was said and done, it was a lucrative day for all three of us. We split the donations and tips evenly, which was fair. There were more than fifty audience members in attendance and all of them donated money to the musicians.

I don't remember how long we played or even how many songs I played but it was probably a two-hour show and we more than likely played around ten original songs each. We told stories and jokes and even had an intermission break where we talked with the audience. It was a cold day and I remember wearing a wool sweater and drinking hot tea. The people in the audience were sitting in their lawn chairs with blankets wrapped around their legs and hot cocoa in their mugs. Here in Tampa Bay, I don't play outside in the cold too often, but that day was fine because there was so much positive energy and everything just went really well for everyone involved.

Have you ever been flipping channels only to find live music? Recently while I was doing just that I came across a Solo Acoustic Musician performing a country song and I stopped to watch the show. As the SAM continued to play, the cameras were panning and switching angles, and they revealed more SAMs on the stage next to him. I don't remember their specific names, but they were four currently famous or touring country artists who were taking turns performing some of their hit songs in the round.

These songs were current on the radio when I saw the show, and I recognized all of them immediately. It was interesting to watch them perform and react to each other's songs. The concert was taking place in a small venue with a stage, lights, and all that it would entail for a performance like this. There was a host who narrated and introduced each act. The artists on stage engaged in a little bit of banter between themselves and each one of them told stories about some of the songs they played. All four of them seemed very relaxed and acted like professional, seasoned performers.

Each member of the group tours with a full band, and it was really cool to see them play the songs stripped down as Solo Acoustic Musicians. Sometimes the essence of a ballad or the feeling of a big hit can get lost in all the lights and smoke on tour.

A great example of what I am talking about is showcased in the movie *Pure Country*, starring George Strait. He plays the main character "Dusty," and his touring show has grown to include a lot of lights, smoke, and all the things we have come to expect from a big concert in an arena or stadium. Dusty comes to the realization that it has all come to be way too much for him and he doesn't like it anymore. He stopped singing in the middle of his big hit song and according to him, nobody noticed because everything was way too loud. He says that he can't breathe right because of all the smoke and that his fans can't even see him because of all the lights that blink all over the place.

Well, by the end of the movie, he ends up doing a stripped-down, solo acoustic version of a new song he wrote. He doesn't even sing it into a microphone and the audience loves it. I don't know if you can tell, but I really enjoy that movie. I have a lot of music-related movies that I like to watch. Oh yeah, back to the round...

These four country singers on the stage were quite entertaining and shared the stage together gracefully. I was engaged by their stories and songs as I sat on my couch. I thought to myself, how cool would it be to be at that concert in the audience? What an intimate way to see and hear more than one top-notch performer do their thing. I don't know how often songwriter rounds like this happen on TV or in the real world on a stage near you, but buying a ticket to go see one would probably be worth your time.

There is a music store in St. Petersburg, Florida, about forty minutes south of my house that focuses on acoustic guitars, and also has a stage and has become a music venue. This shop is home to a team of luthiers and is owned and led by a father and son. The dad spent something like thirty years working as a top luthier at Taylor Guitars. In the store, they have built a coffee and snack bar area as well as a stage. They host a monthly singer-songwriter in the round event and encourage original songwriting in the local community. Over the course of several years they have become a staple of the Tampa Bay music scene. They are more than just a little guitar shop and have grown into something special. I get text messages and see their flyer posts about their events on social media. They charge a door fee or do ticket sales and have limited seating for the concerts they put on. When I see the pictures and videos from their events, I think it's awesome. Unfortunately, I am gigging so much that I have not been able to attend one of the concerts yet. If I do make it then I will tell you about my experience. It is nice to know that these kinds of events are happening in my area. A music scene should have all kinds of venues, types of shows, and styles of events. If you don't have a monthly event in your area, maybe you could start one and find a venue appropriate to host it in.

# CHECK IT OUT FIRST

Over my time as a Solo Acoustic Musician, I have met a lot of other SAMs. I have had many conversations about music, gigs, and the lifestyle in general. Practicing, playing gigs, and going to open mics are common topics that come up in those conversations. As a player and as an open mic host, I have met many SAMs who practice their songs just to play them at open mic events. Practicing songs in preparation for an open mic can be a part of growing as a Solo Acoustic Musician.

I have even met SAMs who only play their songs at open mic events and don't go out and do gigs on their own. These people usually have jobs or are retired and enjoy the music scene from that perspective. The open mic is where they go to socialize and share their songs. Some of them will only play original songs that they have written.

I have seen SAMs start their careers by going to open mics. They start out by practicing their songs at home and picking out three songs to perform. Over time they add more songs and get on stage to play them. It is a way of getting their feet wet and gaining some experience performing in front of an audience.

Something that I have been known to do, and I have seen other SAMs do it, too, is to go to the open mic with the express purpose of just checking it out first. I will not even bring my guitar with me when I just want to get a sense of the vibe. The host, the PA, and the venue are all things I look at when I do this. I want to watch how the host runs the sound and how they interact with the musicians.

I also want to listen to the other musicians and maybe even meet some of them as well. I may have prepared to play but still want to check out the event before I commit to signing up to perform. Sometimes I will bring my guitar, but leave it in my vehicle so that I don't feel obligated to take part. If I change my mind, I can always sign up, get my guitar and wait my turn. I want to be comfortable and this is part of my process sometimes.

I highly suggest going to an open mic just to check it out, especially if you are still working on your music. If you have more than one open mic in your area, then my advice is to visit each of them when you can. You might feel more comfortable at some than others. I like to think of it as going undercover just to see how things are done in each place.

A listening room in St. Petersburg about forty minutes south of my house used to have an original music-focused singer-songwriter open mic every Tuesday evening. This event attracted some pretty good Solo Acoustic Musicians and there was almost always some top-notch talent in the room. It ran weekly for many years, and I used to go regularly at a certain point. At that time, Tuesday was my only night off and I went to support the venue and the event.

It was a really nice venue with a stage, lights, and a wonderful house PA system. The owner also had a recording studio in the back and many really good Solo Acoustic Musicians would frequent the place. They held ticketed shows all the time on Thursday, Friday, and Saturday nights. When I started going on Tuesdays I would sign up and play my three songs. I was very used to playing in front of people for a living but for some reason, I would get very nervous when I took the stage at this venue. My left hand would start to shake and I would struggle to make it through my songs. I started overthinking the situation and couldn't seem to stay calm when it was my turn to play. I would love to say that I never get nervous, but I will admit to you that it happens from time to time.

I had to understand what was happening and I put some effort into analyzing the situation. My conclusion was multi-faceted; I believe several things were happening subconsciously. I was not used to a listening room environment, and it probably weirded me out because everyone was very quiet and looking at me while I was on stage. As a gigging Solo Acoustic Musician, I am more used to the restaurant and bar atmosphere where people are watching TV, talking to each other over drinks, and socializing. I become part of the background. I am not saying nobody pays attention to me in those places, but I am not usually under a microscope or the main focus of every single person in the room.

Another part of it was that I am sure my body and mind realized on a certain level that the other musicians in the audience were top-notch players and that made me more nervous than usual. My hand doesn't start shaking at my normal bar gigs. The audience is made up of random strangers who are probably not awesome musicians. Now I know there will be some good musicians in the audience at my normal gigs, but I probably don't know if they are there or who they are so it doesn't matter.

Signing up on the list was another factor that I didn't realize was contributing to my nervous response on the stage. By the time I was arriving at the venue, I would be the tenth or more to perform. So I was sitting, waiting, and watching a lot of good musicians play their sets. It was a slow build-up of nerves that would of course climax when it was my turn. All of these things were happening, and I wanted to figure out how to get comfortable in this venue. I wanted to conquer my nervous energy and perform at a high level when I returned to this open mic night.

I decided to make some changes. The first thing I did was that I stopped bringing my guitar. After all, at the time, it was my one night off every week and I could just go to hang out. I would show up without my guitar, grab a seat at the bar, order some food and have two beers. I would be quiet, pay attention, and clap after every song. The owner and the bartender both offered to let me use their guitars many times and I declined every time.

Eventually, I came up with something to say to them, and they both laughed and agreed. I told them every great chef loves a good home-cooked meal prepared for them by family and every great masseuse loves a good back rub by someone special. I told them that I enjoyed listening to music as much as I loved to play music and it was my one night off to relax and not play. I explained that I was coming to support the venue by spending money, support the event by being a good audience member, and network with the other musicians. They totally got it and stopped asking me to use their guitars and get on stage. I felt the pressure to perform lessen.

During these weeks when I wasn't performing, I saw the same thing that was happening to me happen to another local gigging SAM. I thought he was really good, and I knew he was working steadily all over town. One time he walked off the stage after his second song and sat in a chair at a front table to play another. He even acknowledged to the crowd that he didn't understand why he was getting nervous on stage at that moment — that he had just played gigs five days in a row and didn't get nervous once.

When he was done and had put his guitar away, I asked him to step outside with me to talk. We grabbed a table out front on the sidewalk and he lit up a smoke. We talked for at least half an hour about how we were both getting nervous at this specific venue. It almost felt like quicksand in that the more we tried to not be nervous, the more nervous we would get and it would just keep getting worse.

Another thing I started doing was arriving earlier, and it clicked one day when I realized that some of the other SAMs were consistently coming every week and signing up in the first five spots before anyone else had the chance. It was then that I decided I was going to sign up in the third slot on the list every week for a while. The list was on a dry-erase marker board that was hanging on the wall next to the green room door and the front-of-house mixing board.

Over about ten weeks, I became a lot more comfortable in this venue. I knew more people, I was familiar with how things were done, and I fit in with the vibe of the event. The more times I went, the more settled into the scene I felt. After this stretch of not playing, I started bringing my guitar again. I would sign up third every week so that I didn't have to wait a long time and that alleviated my self-doubt. They actually stopped erasing my name every week and the third spot on the list just kind of became my spot. I decided to not have any alcohol before I performed, and I would wait until I was done to have a beer and some food while I watched the rest of the SAMs play their songs. I was playing well and I wasn't getting nervous.

For many months after that, I enjoyed going to that open mic. When I look back, I think it would have served me well to just go hang out for a bunch of times before I ever played in that room. For some reason, I believe I should have checked it out first, and I learned a valuable lesson that would come in handy at open mic events in the future. As I always say, every person and every situation is different, so I hope you enjoyed my story and find some value in it.

I have written before about going to an open mic at a brewery where I ended up being twenty-sixth on the list, waited four hours to play, and then broke my low E string at the beginning of my first song. In hindsight, I think I should have gone to that open mic a few times to check it out first. If I had gone there as part of the audience a few times and met some of the other musicians, I might have developed more comfort with the vibe of the event.

I have always thought that my subconscious made me break that low E string, because I never went back to that brewery for their open mic night. I just kept thinking something was off between me and that venue. Even years later when I played two shows there, I didn't like it and although the owner's son, who was in charge of booking the entertainment calendar, wanted to book me again, I declined his offers because I just didn't feel that I was a good fit. I don't know why and I can't explain it but I never felt good in the room.

I wonder if things would have been different if I had gone there to check it out first or if I would have picked up on the negative vibe I was feeling and just avoided playing there altogether. I can't sit around second-guessing my choices from back then, but I do know that I can always go check out an open mic first before I ever sign up and play any songs. It has just become part of my personal process for open mic events.

I have one last reason for you to check it out first that I want to add. It can be advantageous to make sure to initiate contact with the owner or venue representative who is in charge of booking the venue's calendar before you ever sign up on the list or play any songs on the stage. If you're trying to get a gig at the venue and you playing at the open mic is supposed to be an audition of sorts, then you want the person who is in charge of booking to see you perform.

When I first moved to Florida, I was very active in going out to places to talk to people about playing in their venues. One of the first places that I visited told me that they booked talent from the musicians who attend and perform at their weekly Wednesday open mic night. So I planned to go the following week and try out. Between that day and the next Wednesday, I did find a Wednesday gig that ultimately lasted for four years, starting in two weeks. So I would have just that one Wednesday evening to go to this open mic and I hoped that the owner, who was in charge of the calendar, would like me and book some dates.

I arrived, I signed up, and I waited to play my three songs. When the host called my name and I took to the stage, I noticed that the owner went behind the bar and disappeared through a door into the kitchen. I had talked with her after I signed up to play and I had made sure she remembered me from our previous conversation days earlier and that she knew I was there for the express purpose of showcasing my talents in hopes of booking some dates. It was like magical timing when right after I finished my performance she reappeared from the back to her seat at the bar. I sat at my table watching other Solo Acoustic Musicians perform their songs and I clapped for them.

A little while later, I made my way over to her to chat, and her response to my request of booking a date or two was that she didn't see or hear me play and that I should come back again the next Wednesday night. I was polite and told her that I had just booked myself every Wednesday for the foreseeable future.

She still didn't book me.

On the drive home, I considered the idea that it was just part of her strategy to get musicians to return and fill her open mic list. I wondered how many more weeks I would have to show up before she would stay in the restaurant to watch me perform. I would have totally expected her to do the same thing the next week. I didn't want to chase that carrot anymore, and I moved on to other venues.

I would finally play at that venue nine years later. She actually contacted me because some of her employees heard me perform at another local bar and asked for my card. They told me they wanted me to play at their workplace and talked to the owner. I played there once, and I didn't go back because the owner was rude to me again.

Although this story is an example of when it didn't work out for me, there were several open mic nights where I did get booked after playing my songs. Making contact with the venue representatives was an integral part of making it happen.

After going through some of these weird experiences at open mics and practicing what I preach by checking it out first, I have found that I have a good vibe detector. There have been a few times where I went to an open mic just to check it out and I didn't like the event, so I didn't stay and I didn't go back. I felt completely comfortable leaving and spending my energy on other open mics that were more to my liking. No harm, no foul, check it out first.

 # ETIQUETTE

What is etiquette?

The customary code of polite behavior in society or among members of a particular profession or group.

Etiquette can be vital if you are a player, because if you are not practicing good etiquette you may be asked to leave and not come back. Etiquette is essential if you are hosting an open mic event, because if you protect the players by making sure everyone is following good etiquette, then they won't have a reason to stay away. They will have a reason to want to come to the open mic event that you host.

Remember my story about the bassist and the djembe player who started playing with me against my will? If the host musician had intervened on my behalf and stopped them from "jamming" along with my song, I probably would have gone back to his open mic again. Clearly, for you as a Solo Acoustic Musician, the etiquette lesson from that story is, don't play along with someone who doesn't want you to join them.

A common example of this behavior is when someone in the audience starts playing the harmonica during someone's performance. It happens sometimes, and not exclusively during blues songs, although it is more likely then. It can be a disaster if the harmonica is not the right key for the song, and overall it is rude and disrespectful, so don't be that guy. Another common example of an audience member violating etiquette is playing the tambourine or some kind of percussion instrument during someone's performance. It is not much fun when you are a performer. Can you imagine having your eyes closed and being halfway through your favorite song, only to have someone in the audience start beating a tambourine, badly and off beat? Talk about a distraction.

As a host, I have experienced some rowdy patrons or musicians in the audience. Every now and then, when someone gets a little too drunk and loud in the crowd, I have to go over to their table and ask them to take it down a notch. I always explain that people are trying to perform, and ask them to please respect the musicians. I once had to tell a musician to leave and not come back, because he was acting out and even harassing the other musicians, and I wanted to protect them from his rudeness.

Most open mics are held in a venue that has alcohol available, but it is important not to get drunk or wasted before walking onto the stage. Some open mics are held in non-alcohol-type venues like churches or coffee shops, so that won't be a problem. When I was a host, there were a few times when a musician had obviously had too much to drink and I had to deny them access to the stage. Most of them were subdued and just stayed seated and continued drinking, but there was one guy who got mad, and I had to get the bartender to help me deal with the situation. It was not fun, and I didn't want him to come back anymore, so I made sure to email him the next day and tell him that he was not welcome at my open mic.

Another time, I felt very bad for the guitar player in a duo act. His partner was a bass player and was very quiet, but once he started playing it was obvious that he was drunk or on drugs of some kind. He stood up and was swaying back and forth and then sat back down and was almost nodding off. The guitar player was embarrassed by his friend's actions and returned the next week without him. We discussed it briefly, and I was happy that he came back — and this time he actually sounded good.

Whether you are a musician or a host, keep an eye and ear out for these situations and try to help things end well. It's a challenge to keep the train on the tracks and not have a derailment or accident. A room full of musicians and their egos, along with alcoholic beverages, can even lead to arguments or fights.

It took a while for me to find out why two guys who were regulars at my open mic had stopped coming around, but I eventually found out why. Evidently, they were both at a different open mic and got into an argument and started pushing each other around and had to be separated. Now, neither of them were coming to my open mic because they thought that the other would be there. It sucked for me to lose two musicians who had been attending every week. It wasn't my fault, and I had no control over the situation. All I could do was reach out to both of them and let them know they were missed at my open mic and that I hoped that they would return. Good etiquette dictates that you should not get inebriated and act out like those guys. Stay calm, be cool, and enjoy the music.

As a Solo Acoustic Musician who is attending an open mic event, you should be supportive of every other musician who takes the stage to perform. The best way you can do this is by joining in the applause at the end of each of their songs. Be respectful and quiet while they are playing, pay attention to their performance, and when they finish a song, let them know you appreciate their effort by clapping. Even if you are the only person who is clapping, it's OK because you will probably help get others to clap along. Never heckle any of the other musicians. Don't talk loudly during their performance. Be a part of the group that is doing the right thing and acting with respect and good etiquette. Be patient waiting for your turn to perform. Sometimes it may be a while before you get to go on stage.

As a player, I have had my share of open mic experiences that didn't go well. When I first moved to Florida in 2008, I was looking for gigs and also trying to meet other musicians on the scene, so I went to some open mics.

A local brewery had one every Wednesday and I went to check it out. I called ahead and asked about their event and was told that the list went out an hour before start time, so I arrived a little bit beforehand. When the clipboard with the sign-up sheet was placed on the stage I got in line to sign up. I was fifth in line, and there was only one person behind me. When I got to the clipboard to sign up, though, I was the twenty-sixth name on the list. The people in front of me had signed up a bunch of their friends as well as themselves.

I waited about four hours to get on stage, and when I began my first song I broke my low E string. I just put my guitar in my case, walked off the stage, and went home. About ten years later, I ended up having success playing at that brewery but for the longest time, I had no interest in the place. In my mind, I just felt like something was off between my vibe and the vibe of the venue, so I didn't bother going there again.

The etiquette lesson here is, don't sign up anyone else on the list. In my opinion, the host should have been aware that this was happening, to the point that it had obviously become normal for people to do it every week. So as a player, don't do it and as a host, keep an eye out for it so you can stop it from happening.

When I was hosting open mic night events, I did not allow people to sign up ten other people who were on their way and had not yet arrived. The list should be a first-come, first-served situation. If you are first in line and want to sign up for the tenth spot, though, that should be allowed and I have seen people do it consistently. Sometimes people don't want to be first to play and will choose to appear further down the list.

I once watched an open mic run itself into the ground by filling up the sign-up list before the night even started. If you are the host, and you happen to know 80% of your regular attendees, make a rule that they have to show up 30 minutes in advance like everyone else to claim a spot on the list. Don't let them text you, email you, or social media message you to claim a spot the night before.

This particular open mic got so accustomed to filling the list up that newbies stopped coming because they could never get on the list. Some had even waited outside the venue for an hour, but by the time doors opened, the list was already full. That event quickly earned a bad reputation.

Hopefully, you can become a part of the support system for the open mic event. Part of being supportive is spending a little bit of money in the venue. I bring this up because in my experience as a host, I have had to have conversations with managers and owners about money. One example went like this...

I started an open mic every Monday night and it lasted for three years at the same venue, a small taphouse with no kitchen. When we agreed to launch the event, they were bringing in between one hundred and two hundred dollars on Monday nights. They did have some snacks, but their focus was on craft beer and wine. There were a couple of TVs on the wall above the bar and they had a few games available for people to play.

After a couple of months, I had a meeting with the owner to evaluate the progress of the event, and we were ringing in around eight hundred dollars every Monday. Because of this financial success, I was able to justify my pay as well as build some longevity and consistency for my open mic event. The musicians who were attending were bringing friends and family to hear them play, and everyone was buying something: a bottle of water, a bag of chips, a beer, or a glass of wine. It all added up to a financially successful open mic event and the owner was happy to have us all there playing music.

I have hosted open mics in venues that had kitchens and full menus, and that helps a lot, especially if you have players who do not drink alcohol, but that will be discussed later. The point I am making in regard to etiquette is to buy something in support of your host and the venue. If you get a cup of coffee, an iced tea, or a snack, it all helps keep the event going. The staff will complain if everyone who attends an open mic asks for a glass of water and nothing else.

I have even heard similar conversations between a bartender and a manager about their karaoke night. They complained that the customers and singers who were there for the karaoke night event weren't buying anything and weren't tipping, but they were coming in every week, and taking up tables where paying customers could have been seated.

Another part of showing support for any open mic event is to become a regular. Maybe you can go every week, or every other week, or just once a month. It is vital to any open mic to have musicians come out to perform. You may have more than one weekly open mic event in your local area, and you may like all of them. Each one will be different, and you will probably have a favorite, but variety is the spice of life and going to other open mics can be fun. Even when you are on vacation or out of town for some other reason, you can find an open mic and support the event and perform your music.

No matter where or how often you can go to an open mic, you should try to become friends with the host and join the local network of musicians. They will probably have a social media group page and other SAMs who attend on a regular basis. There is a certain amount of appreciation and camaraderie, both in person and online, in a group like that.

Some musicians like to bring their own microphones and I think it is a great idea, especially with all the germs that are floating around these days. As a host, I always had a few extra microphones ready for the performers. But there were also a handful of people who brought their own microphones. They would tell me they liked the way it sounded, or that they didn't want to sing on the one everyone else was using because the flu was going around. It didn't matter to me what the excuse was, I was more than happy to accommodate them. To be honest, I would prefer if every musician brought their own microphone to an open mic. It just seems like a smart thing to do. So it's not an etiquette requirement, but it is something to think about.

A Solo Acoustic Musician who came to my open mic once or twice a month for a few years made a mistake once by showing up sick. This was a total bummer, because we didn't know and a bunch of us got sick. He said hi to everybody and shook hands with most of the musicians in the room, went on stage and performed as normal, but didn't bring his own microphone, which would become my requirement for him specifically in the future.

After he performed he proceeded to hang out until the end of the event. It was at this point that he started coughing a good bit and said that he hadn't been able to shake off a cold or flu for the previous two weeks. I was shocked and concerned for everyone who had just spent time in the room with him.

I think you can tell where this story is going. A bunch of musicians, their friends, and their families got sick. I had to miss a couple of gigs and even cancel some studio time I had booked months in advance. I was charged the full amount of money for my studio time, because I was canceling at the last minute, and I was not very happy about that or having to reschedule and push my recording back by months. I had been practicing my original songs for the sessions and I had to start all over and wait. The lesson here is, don't be the Solo Acoustic Musician who goes to the open mic event when they are sick with a contagious illness. It is just not cool.

A little extra step in the right direction is to tune your guitar before you go on stage. Yes, you may have to tune in between songs, but if you take the stage already tuned then there is an easier transition between acts and it saves a little bit of time, which is important to the host and everyone who is waiting to play. Bringing your tuner helps because it may be loud in the room. Stepping off to the side or even outside of the venue can sometimes be necessary so that you are not making noise while another musician is performing. Try to be conscious of your surroundings and how loud you are while you get your guitar in tune.

If you have any special gear that you are going to use, it would be a good idea to set it up to the side of the stage. For example, if you are using a songbook or music stand with sheets of paper on it, having that set up and your papers in order will help with the transition into your set. Time is of the essence, and you want to be efficient with your setup and breakdown. If you are using an iPad or tablet and have a microphone stand attachment clip that holds it, then you should be prepped and ready to go. Your pedalboard should be out of the case and ready to be plugged in. Maybe you are going to use a harmonica and an around-the-neck harmonica holder. Having your harmonica already out of the case and in the holder will make things smoother than doing that on stage between songs one and two. Thinking ahead and being prepared will be appreciated by the host and the other musicians.

How should you dress for an open mic?

If the venue is informal (most open mic nights and bookstore or café readings are), feel free to wear a good pair of jeans, a "business casual" top, and seasonal yet comfortable shoes. For a more formal setting, you might opt for your best shirt and slacks or a dress.

The majority of open mics I have attended and hosted were in pretty casual settings and wearing whatever you wanted was basically OK. When it comes to wardrobe, everyone has their personal take. I have talked about wardrobe in the previous books in this series, and those words apply here as well. You can base your choice of what to wear on what kind of venue the event will take place in. If the open mic is in a restaurant or a dive bar then you can dress accordingly. I've never been to an open mic in a fancy restaurant where you would need to dress up, but by all means, you can dress up if you want to, right? Sometimes people develop a character and dress a certain way to enhance that character.

I'm aware of a guy with a pirate theme who only drank rum, and he always wore a special hat, a particular shirt, and specific shoes. Sometimes he would even bring a parrot with him. The parrot would sit on his shoulder the whole time. He wrote his own songs and they all had beach, boat, ocean, and pirate themes. I don't think it would matter where or what kind of venue the open mic was being held, he would dress up as the pirate character that he created.

I was usually casual in my clothing choices when I attended open mics and would dress venue appropriate. If you are presenting original material and want the audience to take you seriously, you may want to make an effort to dress a little more than basic casual. The old clichés of "dress to impress" and "dress for the job you want" apply. So if you want to be a rock star or a folk singer or a jazzy-bluesy singer-songwriter, then you can find part of your identity by choosing what to wear when you perform your songs.

There have been quite a few times where someone has said things to me like, "If we didn't just see you on stage we would not have guessed you were the talent tonight," or "We heard you and then turned around and it wasn't what we expected." They were judging a book by the sound of it, if you get what I mean. Because when they saw me, they were judging me by my appearance and making assumptions about what I "should" sound like based on the way I looked. According to them, I should have sounded different than I did based on my appearance. If you take this into account and you want people to accept your music in a certain way for a particular reason, then your appearance can play a critical role in your presentation.

Dressing the part means that if you play heavy metal, then you need to look like it. If you play country music, you need to wear those kinds of clothes. If you want to be taken seriously and accepted in the blues community, it might help you achieve your goal if you dress like a blues musician. I don't believe it should matter, and I do believe that your music should speak for itself, but the public as a whole relates the way you dress to the way you sound. My best advice is to dress comfortably, dress the way you want, and make sure you dress appropriately for the situation, event, and venue.

I have written up a list of possible rules to follow and their application in the "Hosting An Open Mic" chapter. Following the rules laid out by the host is definitely appropriate. To me, etiquette also includes being nice, polite, and just a good person in general. Not every Solo Acoustic Musician who regularly attends the same open mic event is going to become best friends with everyone else, or even like each other, and that is OK as long as there is a basic mutual respect. Just be kind and share in the event. It is OK to not like everyone else's music, but you should still clap for them. It takes a lot of guts just to get up on stage, so be nice. The old adage of "do unto others as you would have them do unto you" could be applied here, because I think you also want everybody to clap for you after you play your songs. The point of an open mic event is to have fun and share in a musical community. Be a part of that community and practice good etiquette.

 # TYPES OF LISTENING

Have you ever noticed someone in the audience watching you in a different way than everyone else there? Sometimes I will talk to a person like that on a break, or call them out from the stage and ask them one of a few different questions. What instrument do you play? What kind of guitar do you have? What type of music do you play? I tell them that I think they are a musician by the way they are watching and listening. Most of the time I am right in my assumption, and it breaks the ice and starts a conversation.

Musicians as a group pay attention, watch, and listen differently than the rest of the audience. Have you ever been to a concert and noticed the musicians watching the show while a lot of other people are dancing? It also happens at my solo gigs in bars and restaurants. Sometimes I miss it or don't engage the person, but between songs or when I go on a break they might approach me and ask a question.

"Is that a Martin? I have a Martin too."

"What model Martin is that?"

"How long have you been playing guitar?"

"What are the pedals you are using?"

Listening to other musicians perform at an open mic is an important part of the event, so let's dive into a conversation about the types of listening and see what we can learn together. I have done some research and compiled some information for us to dissect.

There are different types of listening skills used in human communication. However, in addition to the sound of the message, visual stimuli is also processed, as is information about the sound source and the social situation.

The three main types of listening most common in interpersonal communication are:

Informational Listening (Listening to Learn)

Critical Listening (Listening to Evaluate and Analyze)

Therapeutic or Empathetic Listening (Listening to Understand Feelings and Emotions)

Listening is a conscious activity based on three basic skills: attitude, attention, and adjustment. These are known collectively as triple-A listening.

Effective listening has three modes: attentive listening, responsive listening, and active listening. Understanding these modes will help you increase your listening accuracy and reduce the opportunity for misunderstanding.

Active listening is perhaps one of the most common forms of listening — it occurs when you're having a conversation and wish to show the person you're talking to that you're engaged and alert.

Active listening techniques include focusing on the intent and purpose of the conversation, paying attention to body language, giving encouraging verbal cues, clarifying and paraphrasing information, asking questions, refraining from judgment, summarizing, sharing, and reflecting.

The three main techniques for active listening are paraphrasing, clarifying, and summarizing. The listening process involves four stages: receiving, understanding, evaluating, and responding.

Two processes are involved in listening. Top-down listening uses background knowledge and contextualizes words to aid comprehension. Bottom-up listening uses sounds, words, and other small units to create meaning.

Being a good listener means focusing on the person who's speaking, not to interrupt or respond but rather just to hear them out. Good listeners may play a passive speaking role in the conversation, but they actively engage with the other person using body language and follow-up questions.

Low concentration, or not paying close attention to speakers, is detrimental to effective listening. It can result from various psychological or physical situations such as visual or auditory distractions, physical discomfort, inadequate volume, lack of interest in the subject material, stress, or personal bias.

Active listening is when you are fully aware and concentrating on what is being said, rather than passively hearing what the speaker is trying to convey. The goal of active listening is to acquire information and listen to understand people and situations before responding to them. Active listening requires you to listen attentively to a speaker, understand what they're saying, respond and reflect on what's being said, and retain the information for later. This keeps both listener and speaker actively engaged in the conversation.

A responsive or reflective listener encourages the speaker to continue talking through nonverbal and verbal cues like nodding, smiling, leaning towards the speaker, or saying "Uh-huh," or "I see."

Appreciative listening means we are listening for pleasure, like when we are tuning our attention into a song we enjoy, a poetry reading, actors performing in a play, or a sitcom on television.

In critical, analyzing, or evaluative listening, we carefully consider what the speaker is saying and evaluate whether the information provided is correct or incorrect. In these situations, the listener offers an interpretation of the speaker's message.

Empathic listening is the practice of being attentive and responsive to others' input during a conversation. Listening empathically requires making an emotional connection with the other person and finding similarities between their experience and your own so you can give a more heartfelt response. This type of listening is driven by emotion. Instead of focusing on the message spoken through words, the listener focuses on the feelings and emotions of the speaker in order to process these feelings and emotions.

Instead of relying on words, discriminative listening focuses on tone of voice, verbal cues, and other changes in sound. It is how babies understand the intention of a phrase before they can understand words. People can understand emotions of lyrics even without knowing the language that the words are being sung. An example would be how people talk about going to an Italian opera and being moved by the music and mood without knowing the words.

Comprehensive listening involves understanding the thoughts, ideas, and message. It requires that the listener understand the language and vocabulary. Comprehensive listening builds on discriminative learning. If you can't understand the sound, you will not be able to interpret the language.

Silent listening is a group facilitation technique, often used to avoid reporting back and to encourage multiple perspectives to form at an early stage in the conversation, as well as encouraging deeper listening and scanning for information. It is a stand-alone method, but can also be a component of other methods. The silence that may occur when actively listening allows you to hear the other person's thoughts instead of your own. When you engage in active listening, you can hear more of what the other person is saying and understand their thoughts, instead of forcing your thoughts immediately into the situation.

Paraphrasing is restating the same information, using different words, to more concisely reflect what a speaker has said. It tests your understanding of what you've heard by communicating your understanding of what the speaker said, restating the speaker's thought in your own words.

Deep listening occurs when you're committed to understanding the speaker's perspective.

Full listening involves paying close and careful attention to what the speaker is conveying.

Informational, Informative, or Workplace listening is used to learn and understand information or a message. It requires the listener to eliminate distractions, to focus and take notes or record the speaker to aid in the retention and recall of the information. This type of listening is commonly used in the workplace.

Dialogic listening serves to orient participants in a joint activity where you all work together to construct an understanding of the conversation or issue. In this form of listening, the focus is on what is happening between the participants, rather than each person trying to determine what the other is thinking.

Biased listening is also known as selective listening. Someone who uses biased listening will only listen for information that they specifically want to hear. Some people listen for the guitar part or the lyrics specifically.

Questioning and Advising lets you hear the information you really need to understand, as long as you are actively listening. You may not like the answers, but you need the information to move forward! It is impossible to fully resolve a problem if you don't fully understand the issues first. Advising is the most common listening response, but should generally be used only when the speaker asks for advice, either by asking a question or when they announce a problem. This demonstrates that the speaker is willing to listen and consider your input.

Supportive listening is a technique that enables a person to demonstrate concern during a conversation. Whether it is a client, a friend, or even a co-worker, supportive listening can deepen connections in addition to defusing and clarifying thoughts.

In Active Listening, listeners are encouraged to "listen for meaning," often in terms of a feeling, to guess at that feeling, and then feed it back to the speaker. In Supportive Listening, listeners should not guess at feelings, but work with what's been explicitly put out there by the speaker. It can be easy or a challenge to understand a songs message.

An example of supportive listening might be a brief verbal affirmation like "I appreciate the time you've taken to speak to me," an open-ended question like "I understand you aren't happy with your new guitar. What changes can we make to it?" or asking a specific question like "How many gigs did you book last year?"

Each type of listening has a purpose that can be useful in different situations or relationships. Do we listen differently when we are having a conversation with one person versus when we are in a conversation with multiple people? Do we listen differently when we are talking to someone versus when we are watching someone perform their songs on the stage?

And how does all this listening information apply to our lives as Solo Acoustic Musicians, or in the context of attending an open mic night event?

As audience members, we have to engage in active listening on all levels. Paying attention and using our body language will show the performer that we are listening to their music.

Comprehending the lyrics and being able to discuss them, along with trying to feel and understand the emotional content of the words as well as the sounds of the music, are part of our job as the audience. I like it when someone comes up to me after a performance and points out a lyric that they really liked. It is just as cool when someone asks me, "What did you mean by [insert a specific lyric here]?"

When we actively listen to each person who takes the stage, we can engage in communication with them on many levels. We can stand up and clap really loudly to show our appreciation for a performance that we liked a lot. We can give them a hug to let them know we felt their pain or despair. We can dance to their song if it makes us feel like dancing. There are so many possible responses that are directly derived from listening to and feeling the emotions of the tune.

Now that I have done more research into the concept of listening, I can really appreciate how an audience sits quietly in a listening room setting. They are actively engaged in trying to feel and understand each performer and every single song that they hear.

In an environment like that, it makes sense that when someone started talking, they were shushed very quickly. People who couldn't stay quiet were asked to go outside or leave. In a listening room environment, people are taking listening very seriously, and interrupting that vibe is a big no-no. In a way, it's like meditation, and a loud distraction could interrupt the connection to the emotion.

Songs in general are usually two to five minutes long and that is not a lot of time to get into the feeling of someone else's happiness or pain. Having that interrupted can ruin someone's performance and the audience's chance to feel something. No one involved wants that to happen. Learning to be silent and appreciative of the opportunity to feel what someone else is saying and the emotions their sounds are creating is special. Being a rude loudmouth and ruining the moment for everyone is not cool. Don't be that person!

I know there was a lot of technical mumbo jumbo about listening laid out at the beginning of this chapter, but I hope it has helped you realize how important a part of our Solo Acoustic Musician lifestyle listening is. Even beyond the open mic setting, I always hope for and want people to really listen to me when I am performing. On a recent Saturday evening, I had a whole back porch with twenty-five seats in the palm of my hand. It is a restaurant that I play monthly, and they wanted to try music outside this time. The weather was beautiful and all the seats outside stayed full throughout my three-hour gig. I played straight through without taking a break and a big reason was the audience. They were paying attention. They were receptive. They were engaged. They were responsive.

They were listening to me!

I am not saying they didn't talk at all, or anything like that, but it was reminiscent of a house concert or a listening room and it was happening at a restaurant.

The restaurant is in an old house that was converted, so maybe that helped it feel a little more intimate than a restaurant in a strip mall. That doesn't happen at every gig, and I really appreciate when I am blessed with that kind of audience.

For me, it was like I was playing a private little concert. I was telling stories and projecting the emotions and feelings of the songs. My singing and playing were heightened because I had an actively listening audience. I consider it a treat and I am thankful every time it happens. I made sure to let the audience know how much I appreciated them more than once throughout the evening. A sense of mutual appreciation and gratitude was very present in the moments that were created that night. Even the owners and waitstaff remarked about it to me when I was packing up my gear.

The next time you are at an open mic or a concert, take note of how you and everyone else are listening.

 # NETWORKING

What is a network?

An arrangement of intersecting horizontal and vertical lines. "a spider constructs a complex network of several different kinds of threads"

A group or system of interconnected people or things. "a trade network"

What is networking?

The action or process of interacting with others to exchange information and develop professional or social contacts.

"the skills of networking, bargaining, and negotiation"

The linking of computers to allow them to operate interactively.

"The demand for wireless networking is increasing rapidly"

In the world of SAMs, networking would be the process of interacting with others to exchange information and develop professional or social contacts. So let's talk about building a network and things we can do to start networking with other Solo Acoustic Musicians. The fact is that musicians want to go to open mic nights so they can rub shoulders with other like-minded and talented artists, become a part of their local music community, and be where the action is. The best open mics are not about the best talent. The best open mics are about a great music community.

Open mics are a musician's hangout, so take advantage of the opportunity to talk with them. If you're looking to start a band or find musicians to co-write songs with, there's a good chance they'll be hanging out at an open mic.

I always keep business cards in my car and in my guitar case, so when I attend an open mic, I put them in my pocket and I have some more in my guitar case as well. In SAM 3 I talked about the business card dance, so be prepared to exchange cards with other SAMs at these events. The point is to gather their information and send them a follow-up email and or text message.

If you can establish contact and save their contact information, then it will be easy to access it in the future. Back in the day, I used to bring demo CDs with me to open mic nights so that I could share my original music by giving out some samples to the other Solo Acoustic Musicians. It was also good to have them on hand in case the host or the venue representative asked for one because they wanted to book me. Now I can just email or text them my demo/promo video link immediately.

Another way to go about exchanging contact information is just to ask someone for their phone number and/or email address. Almost everyone nowadays has a smartphone and you can type in someone's information pretty quickly. You can follow that up by sending a text or email immediately to establish a connection.

Some people will see this as a bit aggressive and I agree that it is very direct, but if it feels like it's the thing you should do then by all means go for it. Some musicians who attend open mics are not working gigging musicians and don't have business cards to trade, so this mode of establishing contact would work out best. I still carry a piece of paper and a pen in my pocket and sometimes I just write down an email address. Not everybody has a business card for their job or for any reason at all and being able to get their information in multiple ways allows you to feel out what you think would be most comfortable. Just feel your way around the conversation and try to make a connection. Most musicians are open to exchanging contact information and being a part of the scene or music community.

There can be a lot of benefits to building a network within the open mic world of musicians. For one it will just feel a lot more comfortable when you attend an open mic if you are familiar and even friends with the other musicians in the room. Do you remember that show *Cheers* and how everyone in the bar yelled, "Norm" when he walked in? It feels good to be accepted by the group and feel like you are a part of something bigger than yourself. You may even make some friendships that last for many years or even for life.

As I have mentioned, when I first moved to Florida I started hosting an open mic and I made friends with a lot of local musicians and I am still friends with quite a few of them. There were also times when I went to other open mic events, walked in, and knew a lot of the people there because of my networking when I was a host.

Another benefit of networking at an open mic is being offered gigs. As you become friends with other musicians, you may find yourself being asked to cover a gig for one of them. Whenever a Solo Acoustic Musician is feeling under the weather or going out of town, they usually look to their network of SAM friends to cover their shifts for them. If you are available and can do it, you might pick up a gig. If you have never played the venue before, you might pick up a client. If you can do it, you will be helping a friend and building your relationship with that SAM. They will probably share that information with other SAMs and you will build a reputation as someone who has been reliable in the past when you were asked to help out and cover a shift. Over time this may become a back-and-forth thing where you ask them to cover for you and so on, as you both may need help from each other in the future. As the friendship deepens, they may even offer you gigs that they can't take.

There is one particular SAM with whom I have a reciprocal friendship. I recently picked up a well-paying private party because he was already under contract for a different private function and wasn't available. He asked me if I could do it and put me in touch with the client. I booked the gig and called another SAM friend to cover my bar gig so I could play the more lucrative private party. This type of thing is exactly why we network with other local Solo Acoustic Musicians.

In SAM 2 I interviewed my friend Chase Harvey, and he talked about getting gigs through open mics. When he was a teenager and just starting out, he would frequent open mic nights to perform and network. He was learning a lot and making long-lasting friends in the music scene. He told us about moving to the east coast of Florida and how attending open mic events led to him making friends and getting gigs.

Chase's story is a great example of networking at a musical community event and how it led to positive results. He was able to build relationships with other SAMs which led to covering shifts, getting gigs in new venues, and becoming friends with new people. The very definition of open mic networking is represented in his interview in SAM 2.

You may be looking for a duo partner, and networking at an open mic is a good way to explore options. If you play guitar and sing, and you want to meet someone else who plays guitar and sings so that you can take turns singing lead and sing harmony parts with them as well, then attending an open mic could be the way to find that person. Are you looking for a lead guitar player or are you looking for a singer? Maybe you are looking for someone with whom you can co-write songs. I have seen quite a few duo partners get started at an open mic.

Music is one of those things in our lives that can bring people together, and when two people watch and listen to each other there can be mutual appreciation and respect that leads to sharing a musical experience by playing music together. I consider the Solo Acoustic Musician playing the guitar and singing to be the "anchor," or most common type of musician at an open mic. Other musicians who attend can end up being a duo partner or even part of a group. I had a partner for a couple of years who was a percussionist. He played djembe, cajon, bongos, and other percussion instruments like shakers while I played my songs. We only did three or four gigs a month together, but it was fun to add the rhythm of the drums to my songs.

He went to an open mic that I hosted and told me he was looking to find someone to play with and to get some gigs. In this instance, it ended up working out for both of us and we had fun making music together off and on for a while. I have almost always worked solo, but every now and then I have stepped out of my comfort zone a little bit. The percussion player and I even added a sax player to our act for about six months. We met him at the open mic I hosted, too, and it was a similar situation where he approached me about finding someone to gig with and be a part of the team.

As a Solo Acoustic Musician, I can get gigs on my own but these two guys were unable to pull that off. The term for the kind of musician that they are is sidemen. They look for a person like me or a band to join up with so that they can get on and play gigs. Both of those guys moved out of state, and it ended just as quickly as it started. I have to admit it was fun hearing my original songs with percussion and saxophone. A lot of colors were added to the sound, and I looked forward to when those few gigs a month came up on my calendar.

By going to an open mic and networking with other musicians, you could become an opening act. A lot of lead singers in bands also play guitar and like to perform at open mics as Solo Acoustic Musicians. These people are always on the lookout for other talented musicians, and I have seen SAMs asked to open up for bands. It has happened to me twice, and it was a lot of fun to get to play a forty-five-minute set of my originals at a bigger concert in front of thousands of people.

You never know who will be in the audience at an open mic. Sometimes agents or venue representatives go to open mic events in search of new talent. A young girl who was sixteen at the time I was hosting was offered some gigs and help with booking more gigs by an agent who was in attendance at my open mic. Her parents were with her and helped handle the communication with the agent. She has been gigging with that agent's help ever since.

The venue where the open mic takes place is a potential gig, if you can get the venue representative to listen to your three-song set. By networking with the other musicians at an open mic, you might even get a referral from one of them that helps you get a gig at the host venue. I have asked an owner to pay attention to SAMs I thought they should hire for gigs.

It can definitely pay off to befriend and network with the host of the open mic night event.

Another benefit of networking at the open mic is that you could make contacts who are actively buying, selling, and trading gear. I know one SAM who is still playing the guitar that he bought from another SAM he met at my open mic. There were quite a few deals made among the SAM community that frequented the open mic I hosted. Everyone enjoyed talking about gear all the time. I would constantly overhear conversations:

"What kind of guitar are you using?"

"Check out my new guitar."

"Who is using a [insert brand name] microphone?"

"Is anyone looking to make a trade for some speakers?"

"Check out my new effects pedal. It's awesome!"

There were always conversations like this happening at the open mic. Musicians love to talk about equipment, and SAMs are no exception. Everyone seems to have some kind of brand endorsement or preference. I know Martin and Taylor players who are fanatical. Also, people who prefer JBL, Bose, or Mackie over any other speaker. The gear talk doesn't always lead to buying, selling, or trading but it's still a big part of the communal experience that networking at the open mic creates.

# HOSTING AN OPEN MIC

I will start my discussion about hosting an open mic with a bit about what equipment is needed. As a gigging Solo Acoustic Musician, I always set up equipment to perform by myself. I have scaled down my gear to be quick and efficient with my load-in and load-out. When I was an open mic host, I had to anticipate that some of the acts who sign up to perform might be duos, trios, or even quartets. I ran a singer-songwriter-style open mic, though, so the majority of acts that attended were SAMs.

I liked having one or two main speakers on stands aimed out at the audience. I might only use one main speaker in a smaller venue and two if I was outside or in a larger venue. I would set the height at about ear level for someone standing as I thought that would carry the sound across the top of the crowd when they were seated at their tables.

I applied the same concept to my monitor setup and would use one or two speakers for monitors. At the time, I was using 15" JBL EON 1000-watt powered speakers for both mains and monitors. Those were very versatile because they were built with handles on the sides that made the speakers sit up at an angle on their sides. It was perfect for rolling them over a little bit and sitting up just like a monitor speaker box would be doing. I had four of the same model and they were workhorses for me for several years.

I was using a small twelve-channel mixer and I never needed to use all twelve. It was a Mackie, but I don't remember the model name. I would set up on the side of the stage area so that I could make adjustments and introduce acts without having to walk onto the stage while a musician was performing. I created what I called my "Host Station," and it was where I would run the event from.

When I am traveling around for my own gigs, I only keep one or two mic stands in my van, so when I was an open mic host I would keep four on hand just in case I needed them. As a host who was getting paid and making the weekly event part of the SAM lifestyle schedule on my calendar, I had to invest in a few extra things like extra mic stands, extra cables and extra microphones. I opted to buy Shure SM58s with on/off switches. I found it easier to slide the switch to the on or off position instead of turning the volume all the way down and then back up on the mixer. This way, after I had mixed the levels of the mics during the sound check, I could use the switches to avoid having to make major adjustments on the mixer. I think it made my job a little easier and added some consistency to my mix.

I always had two mic stands and mics set up from the beginning to the end of the event and opted to have the third and fourth sets on standby and ready to go quickly. It was rare that I needed a third or fourth mic. Sometimes when a duo took the stage, both of them would sing. But most of the time, when a trio or quartet came on stage, the added members would not sing. They would usually have an additional instrumentalist playing bass, percussion, keyboard, horn, or violin.

I also provided a quality music stand for anyone who needed one. Sometimes when someone has written a brand-new song, they will bring their lyric sheet with them and need a place to put them so they can read the words off the page. Other times people bring their songbooks. I kept the music stand over to the side unless it was needed, and bought a clip-on light as an accessory. It did come in handy, making people more comfortable when reading their lyrics.

If you get a chance, you should greet people when they arrive and introduce yourself as the host. Doing this can be important to new people who are there for the first time. You will come to know who your regulars are and be able to spot new people quickly. Make them feel comfortable, tell them where to sign up, and go over the rules with them briefly. If you get busy enough setting up or making last-minute adjustments to things around the stage, you might ask a regular to act as your greeter sometimes. You want people to feel included and appreciated, so greeting them can create an atmosphere of acceptance and community.

Where should you put the sign-up list? Some open mics like to have it near the front entrance of the venue, at the welcome station. I have seen it placed near the open mic host station by the stage, at the soundboard, or even placed on the lip of the stage.

I guess it depends how the venue is laid out and how high the stage is. It wouldn't make much sense to lay your list down on the stage if the stage was only ten inches off the ground.

I used to put out the table that I use for merchandise on my own gigs as a table for all things open mic. I had my sign-up list on it, along with business cards and small flyers for the event. I bought a clipboard that I would use just for the sign-up list and loaded it up with copies of a document that I printed out on my computer. It had a header with the title of the open mic, and it said sign-up sheet at the top as well. There were lines for people to sign up with their name, instrument, and email address.

By having people fill in the instrument portion of the list form, I was able to mentally prep for what I would need to do as the host. If it was a duo and it said two guitars, then I would know to be ready to assist with their setup. Along with the other extra gear I had to acquire to be an open mic host, I purchased a bunch of extra instrument cables of various lengths because, as I learned, when extra people take the stage one person will be farther away from the mixer than the other.

Thanks to the email column, I was able to build an open mic email list, and that came in handy when I had to move the event to a new venue. We have a lot of visitors where I live, and it helped me stay in touch with people who came around once or twice a year on vacation or to visit family. I would see a huge pop in my attendance between November and May. When older people up north retire, some of them come to Florida for several months each year. These people are known as snowbirds, and I had quite a few who came out to my open mics.

I grabbed a bunch of other accessories that I thought I might need, like 9-volt batteries for pedals and guitars, a cheap capo or two, individual guitar strings, an extra tuner pedal, picks, an extra guitar strap, an extra string winder, etc...

I even kept extra pens, in case someone took the one by the sign-up list. I attached my pen to the clipboard with a piece of string, but I still kept extras around for when the pen on the clipboard ran out of ink. I wanted to be as accommodating as possible, and if someone came to my open mic and realized that they had forgotten something, I wanted to be able to offer them a replacement if I could. I kept all the extra gear and accessories at my host station.

Once I was prepared with the proper equipment I thought I would need to be a good host, I had to find a venue to stage my event. Remember that old saying, "Location is everything." So I decided to make a checklist of what I wanted my venue to be and why. I knew that not every venue would have all the amenities that I wanted, and I did work with some that did not check all my boxes, but when I worked with the few that had it all, those were the most successful open mics that I ever hosted. I will try to re-create a checklist of things I would want in a venue if I were to ever host an open mic again.

First of all, I would like a stage. A stage makes the performers feel special and more awesome so that would help increase attendance. A stage also makes the performers look cooler to the audience.

Some open mics I have been to and hosted did not have an actual stage and those events were missing something. Moving a table out of the corner of a restaurant and setting up a live music performance there doesn't have the same panache as a stage. I have done it, and I still do perform SAM gigs in the corner, but man, do I love it when I get to be on a stage.

A venue with a stage might also provide some PA equipment. Although this can be rare in my experience, it does happen and finding a venue with some gear would be great. I did host an open mic at a restaurant that had a stage with main speakers attached to the upper corners of the stage and housed in protective boxes. This venue was fifty percent outside and the stage was on the back patio. It had a roof and some flaps to drop in case of weather. I was able to park right next to the stage, which was good for load-in and -out, plus it was extra good for emergency weather load-out. I didn't have to put up main speakers every time and that was cool. But a full-house PA system is ideal and a bit of a dream scenario for an open mic host. Any of the other gear like mic stands would be a bonus. Venues that have a stage, PA, and the other gear you need do exist. I would think, more than likely, the owner of a place like that would be a musician.

Secondarily, I want a kitchen that puts out a full menu of good food. I used to host an open mic at a taphouse that only provided snacks. I have also been to open mic nights in dive bars that didn't have food at all. What I noticed was that some open mic players would have a group with them and not buy anything, or much more than a bottle of water. They had all gone to the restaurant next door for dinner and drinks right before coming to the open mic. I think they would have had dinner and drinks at my open mic if the venue had food.

By having a kitchen with good food I, as a host, would be able to increase the venue revenue on my night, give my open mic musicians an amenity, and make my venue representative happier with my event.

Along with food is a full bar, and what I mean by that is having beer, wine, and liquor available. When I was hosting at the taphouse I mentioned before, all we had available for customers was beer and wine. No kitchen and no hard liquor. I learned that some of the musicians would sneak in their own liquor in miniature bottles, or in water bottles mixed with soda pop. Some of them told me they wouldn't be coming back because there wasn't liquor, that they would be going to a different open mic that had liquor and took place on the same night of the week.

One very specific example was the musician I mentioned earlier who had a pirate theme to his name and act. He only drank rum, and he wanted rum when he went out to perform at open mics, so he wasn't interested in coming back to that taphouse for that specific reason.

In addition to having a kitchen and full bar, I would want the owner or manager to work out a food and drink special for my night of the week. Any kind of deal to entice people to attend an event will help. Remember, the open mic is probably going to be on a Monday, Tuesday, or Wednesday night, and some specials on those nights are always a good idea.

A venue that makes the open mic the focus of the night will become a destination spot for people looking for something to do on an off night. Good turnout is all about the partnership between venue and host. Pick a spot that cares just as much as you do. This is key.

A coffee shop, restaurant, or other space that cares about the local music scene will not only make more money from patrons, but they will help your open mic become better. They will support you by offering drink specials and discounts to attendees as incentives to come out, and visitors will become regulars. Find a listening room, coffee house, brewery, winery, restaurant, church, bar, or pretty much anywhere with a receptive owner who will pay you to be a host.

In SAM 1 I wrote about vertical employment on the gig calendar. When looking a for a venue to host a successful open mic, my goal would be to fill in a weekly Monday, Tuesday, or Wednesday evening. This would vertically fill in a day of the week on my calendar. With a weekly residency like this, I can develop a consistency that customers and musicians can count on. It is just another part of finding the best venue for my open mic night. Believe it or not, some venues will try an open mic on a Friday or Saturday, and those are nights when I prioritize my well-paying SAM gigs.

I also avoid hosting an open mic every other week. Some venues don't want to commit to a weekly event, but I don't like the every-other-week or once-a-month model. It is harder to advertise and to get people to consistently attend. Musicians will show up on the wrong week and get discouraged about coming back again. I want to make getting people in the door as easy as possible for myself and the venue. Inconsistency is an obstacle to my success as a host.

In the past, I have been willing to cut my fee in order for the venue to fill in a weeknight slot like every Monday night. I am no longer willing to make that sacrifice, and this is why. Running an open mic takes more work than any of my Solo Acoustic Musician gigs. That extra work adds stress to my life and takes up more of my personal time. All the worry over getting people to the event and the amount of effort it takes to constantly promote it are worth being paid a normal base rate at minimum. There should be no discount or concession made just to fill in an off night at the beginning of the week. But like I said, I have accepted that deal in the past, so I am not telling you not to if you need to make that money.

Getting paid $100 or $150 every Monday can be better than making $0 on that night. If your base fee is $200 and you turn down a $150 counteroffer to stick to your guns, then you have to be willing to accept it if they decide to pass on your sales pitch for the event. In this world, almost everything can be negotiable, but you have to do what is right for you.

When preparing your pitch to a potential open mic venue, consider the amount of time the event will last. My preference is three hours. I have seen a four-hour open mic be successful but the successful ones I have encountered usually top out at three hours. You can always keep going if four hours' worth of people sign up, but it is no fun dealing with an owner who expects four hours of music when you only have five people on the list.

Planning and promoting a three-hour open mic is best in my opinion. The musicians will know that they won't have to wait forever to get their chance to play. On a night with seventeen people on the list, chances are you will go over three hours but not all the way to four. If each player gets ten minutes, eighteen people can perform in three hours. Now adjust to allow for every person getting on and off the stage, moving mic stands around, the occasional little bit of extra time if their third song goes past the time limit and it's really fourteen or fifteen musicians.

The ten-minute or three-song rule is really more of a guideline that should allow everyone to get a somewhat equal and fair amount of stage time. A person can get a second turn if your list is light. For example, if there are nine or ten people on the list and you still have forty-five minutes scheduled for your event, then you can recycle the list and ask people if they want to play a couple more songs.

As you can see, each item on this checklist is important for a reason. Having them all is my goal if I am going to host an open mic. I would be able to accommodate everyone and have everything everyone might need. I want to give them every reason to come to my open mic, and limit or eliminate any reason or excuse for them to avoid or bypass my event.

As the host of an open mic, you're going to need to make some rules. Don't be afraid to make a change if something isn't working, but being consistent and fair is important. Don't play favorites with your friends. Make sure the rules are clearly communicated to the players and audience members. You could print up a sheet of rules and leave it by the sign-up list. You can announce the rules on the microphone. If you have a dedicated website or social media page for your event, it would be appropriate to post your rules there as well.

As a host, you have to follow your own rules. There's no point in making them if you don't follow them. Lead by example for everyone else. Don't be on the side of the stage, talking loudly on your phone or goofing off and laughing with friends. It is your job for the evening, and it's important that you practice what you preach. If you want everyone else to pay attention to the rules you make, then you have to model the right way to behave.

Look after your equipment or the house PA. Gear is expensive and can be easily damaged by disrespectful people. Make sure you keep your eye on it at all times, and that the performers respect the gear. You may have some regular participants who can help you with this as well. You may need a bathroom break or get distracted by another musician needing help, so having someone else in the audience who is aware of the equipment can help out immensely.

Give performers some notice that they are coming up next. You can do this on the microphone when you are announcing the performer taking the stage. Performers are often there to have a good time with their friends and might not be ready when it is their turn. Give them a shout-out to make them aware that they are up next. It will help to keep things running smoothly.

Make sure performers are on track, and be ready to wrap them up if they are going over their allotted time. Once when I was hosting, a Solo Acoustic Musician just started playing a fourth song right away. He knew the rules and had a smirk on his face that let me know he did it on purpose. His action was seen as rude by all the other musicians at the event. As the host, I had to talk to him about this and decide how I would handle him in the future. I concluded that I would tell him not to do it again or he would be banned from my open mic night.

Don't be negative. Doing things like complaining or talking about any of the musicians behind their backs is not cool. You could develop a bad reputation if people hear you doing these things.

Watch the other performers. You should want to, and the audience members might follow your lead. As the host, you need performers to return, so you want everyone in the room to give them their attention. Being respectful and attentive and paying attention to every player is a good thing to do.

Be aware of those who play and then leave right away. It's poor etiquette and frowned upon by the other members of the open mic community. Sometimes it happens for a good reason, and sometimes musicians are going to more than one open mic in one day.

A tough one to handle can be crowd control. Nowadays, everyone has a phone in their hand. Interference from ringtones, phone calls, or audience members talking loudly can be disturbing to the musicians who are on the stage. As the host, you will have to find a friendly way of asking them to be quiet. You can also make announcements about people turning off their ringer volumes for the event.

As a host, I have always started the open mic by playing three songs. I have been to open mics where the host went right to the first person on the list and then they would just pick a spot whenever they wanted somewhere in the middle of the event to play a few songs. Believe it or not, I have been to some open mics where the host didn't play any songs. They just MC'd the event, ran the sound, and moved everyone on and off the stage.

Something like an MC/Sound Guy/Roadie combination. (The term MC stands for Master of Ceremonies and they announce the stages of the events and keep things organized.) I always started first to be an icebreaker because I wasn't nervous or scared to get up and play a few songs. I thought it would put people at ease and lessen their nerves or anxiety.

 # PROMOTING THE OPEN MIC

When I go to an open mic as an audience member, I can help support and promote the event by bringing a friend. This is the most basic level of promotion, but it is still very important. Word of mouth is valuable. If your friend has fun, they will tell other people, and if you make the audience bigger then everyone who goes to the open mic will have a better experience. The word will spread that the open mic is a happening place to be. Attracting audience members is just as important as attracting musicians.

Most of the time I will call a friend and pick them up on the way or meet them there. For me, it is a social evening out of the house where I am not performing. I also go to see other SAMs play their gigs and sometimes I will bounce around from place to place catching a few songs or a set of each SAM I can find that night. I always try to bring a friend.

As a Solo Acoustic Musician who is going to the open mic to sign up and perform, I definitely want to try to bring friends. I can call or text a few people and even book a reservation for a table if I want to make sure we have a spot. I can also post on social media that I will be there to showcase some new original songs.

It is never a requirement to bring anyone with you to an open mic, but if you can then it helps the event. There is a lot of pressure on the host to get people to show up every week. As a musician who signs up to play, I can tell you I don't want to play my songs for an empty restaurant. I also don't want to play for just the other ten musicians on the list. I want to have an audience, and I hope to have them like my songs and clap for me. I can help assure that that happens by doing self-promotion and reaching out to friends.

Pro Tip

When a new person comes to your open mic, ask them how they heard about your event so that you know which promotions are working for you.

A host must go all the way when promoting the open mic night. Word of mouth via phone calls, text messages, and emails to friends is just the first step. This should be followed by posts on their personal social media pages. Making flyers for print is another step in the promotion of the event. When I made flyers to print out and distribute locally, I wanted to have different sizes.

A standard 8 ½" x 11" piece of paper is good, but cutting that piece of paper into four smaller flyers is a great way to increase your reach. You can place smaller flyers in stacks in the venue, and by the notice board in local music stores. Put an 8 ½" x 11" version on the board and leave a small stack of the others underneath. You can also make one or two poster-sized flyers for inside the venue.

For example, you could put an 11" x 17" poster by the front door or in the front window, and another in the hallway by the bathrooms. These two locations are great spots for flyers and posters, because people have to come through the front door and people need to use the restrooms.

If you have a front window by the front door to work with, then you have the opportunity to hang a two-sided poster. If you put two posters back to back then people will pass it on the way in and on the way out. I will also add that if you do this and your weekly event is going to last a while, then you should have the back-to-back double poster laminated so that it will not need to be replaced all the time.

If you have some local colleges with music departments, you can ask a teacher or staff member about putting up flyers somewhere in the building. They will probably have a community announcement board in a hallway or lobby. You will most likely need to present your flyer and get approval before you can put it up, but it will be worth the effort. College kids who are musicians are looking for events like open mics, and you have a lot of potential players and audience members in the schools.

You can also ask music teachers or guitar teachers specifically to place some of your flyers in their homes or music store areas where they teach. Music students are great candidates for open mics, both as audience members as well as performers. Your flyers can also be used online and on social media pages. Email or message them to other Solo Acoustic Musicians that you know and ask them to share them a couple of times.

When I was an open mic host, I did not have the ability to create a social media group page for my events. Now you can make a group on social media and grow it with musicians who have played at your event. You can add your group name to all your flyers and use the group to share information about the event. Making announcements, putting out a list for early sign-up if you want to do that, and sharing performance videos from your event can all be done on a social media group page.

I have seen nightlife or music scene websites and publications in different cities around the country and I know they are available for musician and band promotion. These outlets will list concerts, theatre shows, and local-level band show dates. From the national to regional to local level, acts will have their shows listed. The venues advertise their calendars on these websites and in these publications. I am thinking of companies like Racket in Minneapolis or Creative Loafing where I live. All things lifestyle will be present including restaurant reviews, things to do, and anything regarding the local music scene.

Where I live in Tampa Bay, there are a couple of websites that promote what's going on around the area. The venue can list upcoming musical acts. The musicians can add calendar dates and share a link with people on social media.

If you want to you can even spend money on advertising on one of these sites. Think about a business card-size ad on the left side of the website in a stack with other musician and venue ads. Maybe you can convince the venue representative to foot the bill for an ad like that. It will be seen by potential audience members and all kinds and levels of musicians looking for events to attend.

Does your local newspaper have nightlife or live music listings of some kind? This is free promotion and shouldn't take much more than a phone call and an email to arrange. Most papers have a weekly listing to let people in the community know what's going to be happening. The newspaper should also include the same list on its website as well. A lot of fans of music or possible audience members, along with a lot of musicians, look at this page in the papers every week.

Back around 2010 I was actively hosting my open mic night in the same venue every Monday evening for a three-and-a-half-year stretch. During that time, I was also playing every Wednesday night for four years straight in a venue that was owned by the same people. These two locations are about eight miles apart but a world away from each other in Pinellas County, where we have a very dense population center. It was a taphouse that served craft beer, wine, and snacks. There was no kitchen, but they permitted and encouraged people to order delivery or bring carry-out with them to the bar.

At the time I was probably about a year into both of those stints with this business. They had been trying music on different nights, booking solos, duos, and bands on the weekend. All of a sudden, they started cutting back on music and I had a thought that helped me stay on the calendar with my two shifts. It worked and I was the only musician working those two rooms for a couple of years before I found another place to move the open mic and a new Wednesday spot that lasted for almost three years.

What did I do? I decided to make a TV commercial. I called up the local cable company and went to their headquarters for a meeting with a fellow who was in charge of sales and placement of commercials. I learned a bunch of information about what I needed to do, and I was also directed to one of their former employees who could shoot video, do the voice-over, and edit the commercial.

Before I went ahead with making the commercial, I talked with the owners about splitting the cost. I told them that I would foot the bill of $400 to make the commercial and that

I was willing to budget $100 a month to pay for placement. I asked them to match my monthly budget for each location, so that I would have $300 a month to spend on putting the commercial on TV.

I showed them a list of channels and prices and they agreed with me that the best bang for our buck was late in the evening and into the midnight hour on ESPN. Prime time was way more expensive, and we tried to pick a channel that people in our demographic of beer drinkers and musicians would see. ESPN was the obvious choice, because it is almost always on the TV in bars, restaurants, and breweries. The people that would see our commercial would probably be at a bar drinking or be on a gig in a venue that had a TV on the wall.

They agreed to match my budget and I shot the commercial. The ex-employee of the cable company came to both of my events and filmed a bunch of performance footage and B-roll, and his wife did the voiceover. A couple of weeks later, we had a finished commercial to present to the cable company. It was professionally done with all the technical parameters that were needed, like the colored bars that have to be there at the lead into the commercial.

We ended up running the commercial for a couple of years, and it was always cool when someone would tell one of us that they saw it. It advertised both of their locations and my Wednesday gig. The commercial also pushed my open mic. It was particularly awesome when someone new came out on a Monday night and when I asked how they heard about the open mic they said, "I saw it on the TV."

If I were to become an open mic host today, I probably wouldn't go as far as to make a TV commercial, but I would find someone to help me make an awesome promo video. If

I had to pay them, which I am sure I would, I would ask the venue owner or representative to split the cost with me. I would have video footage from the open mic, write a short script for voiceover content, and make it shareable on all social media platforms.

I have never seen a promo video for an open mic night, but I am sure somebody out there has made one before. I think it's a great idea and definitely takes things up a notch from just a flyer, though of course I would still make and use flyers, too. In a video, SAMs can get a feel for the vibe of the venue and the event. Hopefully, it entices them to check it out in person and become a recurring member of that open mic community.

In the next chapter, Find a Local Sponsor, I share some thoughts on getting the venue owner, management team, and all of the staff involved in helping with the promotion of open mic events. If you can get the owner behind you personally and financially, you have a better chance of success and they have a better chance of making a profit from a weekly event.

 **FIND A LOCAL SPONSOR**

Back when I was a host, part of my job was to get musicians to come out to play their songs. I started with the traditional routes of promotion, and reached a point where I eventually began to think outside of the proverbial box of what was typically being done by other hosts. I thought to myself, how can I get a sponsor or sponsorship of some kind that will help my open mic appear cool and increase people's interest in attending? I came up with a few things.

I went around to my local music stores to ask the managers if they would be interested in helping me with my open mic. It didn't take long before I was able to get one of them to give me some gear that I could raffle off at the end of the event. I bought a big roll of raffle tickets and when people would sign up to perform, I would give them a ticket and put the other half in a Tupperware container with a lid on it.

If you don't know how raffle tickets work, each one has a twin attached to it on the roll. You give one ticket to the buyer and hang onto the other. At the time of the drawing, you shake up the container and have a non-biased person reach in and pull out a ticket.

I would not want to be accused of playing favorites if any of my friends won the prize. I was able to get the bartender to reach into the Tupperware and pull out a ticket. This gave people an extra reason to stay until the end, which was good for my event.

Sometimes SAMs will play their songs at an open mic and then leave before the end. I have even seen an open mic where half of the musicians who had signed up and played all left at about the same time, and it kind of emptied the room. They played and the audience paid attention to them, clapped, and supported them, but they did not return the favor for the other musicians on the list.

Although it is not a requirement to stay for the whole event, it does help everyone involved. So the end-of-the-show raffle drawing was going to help me keep people in their seats.

I was able to get small items like guitar picks, string winders, and packs of acoustic guitar strings from the music store, and I offered to include their name and logo on all the promotional materials. My flyers for print and online got a little more exciting with the addition of this information.

Once a month I would be able to raffle off a little bit bigger prize like a ten-dollar capo or a patch cable. The store also gave me stickers, hats, and even a couple of their store T-shirts. I had a box of prizes that would last for months of open mic nights and add some excitement to my event. None of the other open mics in my area were giving away swag of any kind. A one-dollar string winder might seem like an insignificant prize, but like I said, no other open mic was giving away anything.

I have been to open mic nights where the venue gave one free drink to any musician who signed up on the list and played on the stage. They would be given a chip or ticket of some kind and could redeem it at the bar after they played. I was able to talk my venue into working with me and a local brewery to do this, and add their beer as a drink special for one dollar off on the night of the event. So every Tuesday, a local brewery's beer on tap would be discounted by a dollar per pint for anyone in the venue. You didn't have to sign up on the list or play to get the discount. This way the friends and families of the players would also be able to get the dollar off.

Also, anyone who just wanted to go to that venue would be able to get the discount applied to their bill at checkout. Once again, the partnership or sponsorship would liven up my promotional materials and enhance my event. Doing these things helped make my open mic night more interesting for the patrons of the venue. If you had to choose between two different open mics that were taking place on the same night of the week, which one would you choose, the one with a beer discount and a musical gear raffle or the one that didn't do anything special?

In SAM 3 I talked about different sponsorship ideas, and they can easily apply to an open mic night event. You could get a traditional sponsor who trades products or services or pays you money to add their name and logo to your promotional materials. If the venue is a bar or restaurant that sells alcohol, then you might even be able to get an attorney who specializes in DUI law or vehicle accident law to be a sponsor. It may seem a little outside the traditional way of thinking, but it makes sense and it's worth the trouble of making some phone calls or sending out some emails to see what kind of response you get.

I am not telling you to go this far with a lawyer sponsorship for yourself or your open mic, but there is a personal injury law firm near me in the Tampa Bay area who does sponsor more than one band and some pretty big concert events that take place annually. The firm has eighteen offices all over Tampa Bay and I see their billboards along major roads when I am driving to and from gigs.

Car, motorcycle, scooter, wrongful death, and other categories of personal injuries are represented by this firm. Personal injuries can have long-lasting effects including medical bills and car repairs. Their experts evaluate factors like distance, speed, and time to determine liability. The bands they sponsor have a large motorcycle-riding fan base and the firm even has a special page on its website dedicated to bikers. It seems that they have a specialty niche in that category and so it makes sense that they would be involved in events where that demographic congregates.

I don't think this firm would sponsor me on any level. However, you never know, and maybe I should call them about working together.

One of the bands had their band truck wrapped with a band logo and stuff like that. The wrap included a picture of the firm's founding lawyer and its logo along with their phone number. I think that band is well sponsored by the law firm, and I would think that with that kind of commitment, they are partners in several ways. Talk about having a lawyer on retainer for every member of the band.

Adding any kind or level of sponsorship to your open mic only helps build the excitement level about your event. Of the three examples I just gave you, I can't pick a favorite. What would it be like if you could get all three? A music store, a brewery, and a law firm. That would be pretty exciting!

The biggest sponsor that is often overlooked and sometimes the hardest to get to help you is the venue. Believe it or not, I have almost always struggled with getting the owner or manager of the venue where my open mics have been held to put any effort into advertising. It would be great if they provided help and resources, but it can be tough to get them to do even the smallest things. It is almost standard practice for venue owners to put all the responsibility for getting musicians and fans to open mic events on the host.

I have tried to explain to them that ten to twelve percent of the population own and play a guitar. If you use the six degrees of separation concept, then everyone knows some people that play guitar and sing. The bartender, wait staff, and kitchen crew all have a friend or a few friends who could perform at the event. Not all of those people are going to be gigging Solo Acoustic Musicians, and most would likely be good candidates for an open mic night.

I think we all have a friend who sits around the campfire and plays us some songs. They are pretty good, but have a day job they like and don't know hundreds of songs. They don't own a PA system or even have the desire to buy one and try to book gigs. These folks are prime targets to recruit for an open mic. If an owner or manager hires you to run an open mic, they should want to get their friends to come and play their songs.

On the other hand, when the person who is paying you to host their weekly open mic supports you by being your biggest sponsor, the event has a high probability of success. Get them to send you their logo and information for the promotional materials. Convince them to share flyers on the venue's social media accounts, as well as their personal media accounts if they have them.

Make sure they add your event to all of their calendars. That could be on a chalkboard or small signs on each table (known in the trade as "table tents") or the spot in the venue where they list their weekly happenings. This type of advertising typically includes food and drink specials, and other events like karaoke and trivia. They should also include your open mic night.

If you are thinking about becoming a host, or already are one, and never thought about getting a sponsor or two or three, now you have a new mission to accomplish, one that will absolutely improve your event. Good luck!

GOING UNDERCOVER

I wanted to go to open mics and investigate — watching and listening to how people act, and how the host does their thing. It had been a long time since I hosted one, so I wanted to see for myself how it's being done now. Part of me wished I was in a movie and had access to the makeup trailer. I could have worn a mask or that rubbery substance they use to age people, put on a wig and turned into an old man to be able to go undercover as a "character" of sorts. Alas, I went as myself.

I used the notes app on my phone so it looked like I was talk to texting with someone. My mission was to see how well the open mics I visited were attended and hosted. I also took note of the PA, the order of the events, and the venues.

I am hoping that each experience will be a story and an adventure because most of the venues are places that I had never been to before. It had been a long time since I had been to an open mic, and I was excited to see what kind of musical acts showed up to play.

PESKY PELICAN

I've asked my friend Rocky to come to some of these open mics with me. On the drive to the Pesky Pelican, I explain that I'm going undercover and not bringing a guitar because I'm not going to play. I don't want him to tell anybody what I'm up to, so they won't be nervous while performing. I'm trying to be very covert and sneaky.

He picks me up at about 5 PM and we drive south for about 50 minutes to the Pesky Pelican. He has a guitar with him, so it looks like I am tagging along.

The host of the open mic is setting up his equipment when we arrive. His name is Tom, and he takes a minute to say hi to us. On our way there, I called Mark Hanson, whom I interviewed in SAM 2, and he may be joining us, so we pick a table in the shade and order some iced teas. Another guy approaches us with a clipboard, paper, and pen. He turned out to be the bass player and clearly a friend of the host. Rocky signs up to be first on the list.

There's one other musician here, a percussionist, and she's very lovely to talk to. She tells us that she networks and sits in with several different local bands, duos, and SAMs. The bass player is setting up a bass amp at stage right . There is a powered mixer and a Behringer speaker with a 12-inch woofer and a horn. It is elevated on a speaker stand to the right of center stage.

The host comes over and introduces himself, asking us if we play guitar together. He's very cordial.

It's an outside venue and extremely hot. The sun will be going down, but they've turned on all the fans to get the air moving.

I have no idea how many people to expect. They have an open mic here every Monday night from 6:30 to 9 PM. The first and third Mondays are hosted by one person, and the second by another person, and this guy named Tom is here to be the host on the fourth Monday of the month.

Another lady has shown up with a djembe, so evidently we'll have multiple percussion players, which is cool and something different.

Rocky starts early and plays from 6:00 to 6:30. Next the host takes the stage and is playing solo. More musicians are arriving and now we have four or five more guitar cases out on the patio. There are a few tables with people who are just here for food and drinks, and everybody's trying to get a nice spot in the shade with the fans blowing on them. The sun goes down around 8:00 at this time of year.

A bass player joins the host, who is playing acoustic. The djembe-playing woman has joined them as well. Her drum is miked up at the bottom. This has turned into an open jam and they're having fun playing, but it's a little different than what I expected or thought it would be, based on their advertisements. There are more people in the audience now, and it is dinner time. It is getting a little bit busy and everybody is having a good time.

A guy shows up with a rather interesting guitar case and takes out a Turkish instrument that I thought was a bouzouki at first, but after talking to the owner I learn it's called a baglama. He has his own guitar amp and joins the jam with this unique instrument. We talk about the Chapman Stick and the Drumatar.

The bağlama or saz is a family of plucked string instruments, long-necked lutes used in Ottoman classical music, Turkish folk music, Turkish Arabesque music, Azerbaijani music, Balkan music, Kurdish music, and Armenian music. It is played in several regions of the world including Europe, the Balkans, the Black Sea, the Caucasus regions, and many countries including Syria, Iraq, Iran, and the Balkan countries. Like the Western lute and the Middle Eastern oud, it has a deep round back, but a much longer neck. It can be played with a pick or with a fingerpicking style known as şelpe. In the music of Greece, the name baglamas is given to a treble bouzouki, a related instrument.

It is now too loud to talk without hurting our voices.

A couple more guitarists show up and sign up on the list. The next act is an acoustic duo. The bass player is helping with hosting duties, introducing some musicians in the crowd who are local celebrities and announcing the food specials and the names of the waitresses. He is definitely running the event.

The bass player and the djembe player begin playing along with the two acoustic guitarists. I was wrong about it being just a duo.

They're having some cable and feedback issues. One of the guitar player's guitar straps breaks, so we're curious to see how they'll respond and keep going. The host brings him a chair and lowers the microphone for him so he can play seated without a strap on his guitar. They make some adjustments and pull it together.

For a moment I think the next performer will be a solo acoustic musician, and I'm looking forward to seeing what he's going to offer, but it turns out to be another jam as the bass player and the baglama guy are back and they are waiting for the djembe player to return.

Some more guitar players have signed up. So now we have about 35 people on the patio. I haven't looked at the list to see how many are signed up, but I count about 14 or 15 musicians.

This is a very loosely run event; there don't seem to be any rules. Everybody's doing four, five, or six songs. Ten-minute jams are the norm. But they are trying to play songs, so it's a very loose format.

Finally, we have our first solo acoustic musician. She asked the others not to join in, and they are respecting her request. There's a lot of feedback but the host is tweaking the P.A. The performer is playing what I think is an original song and she has a very nice voice. She is not using a guitar pick but she is not finger-picking, either; it's more of a light strum and a soft pretty voice. Nice lyrical content. She tells a little story about writing that song, and goes into some finger-picking for a new song she just wrote. She says she's not used to standing, so that's her excuse if she makes any mistakes. I clap for that because I think it's cute and humorous.

She is really nervous and asks for a chair because she's shaking. She's demonstrating some stage fright , but she does sound good sharing her original songs and we are enjoying her music. She settles down and plays a beautiful original ballad in a finger-picking style.

It occurs to me that there is no pad clip/holder on the mic stand, or any kind of music stand for the musicians to use if they needed one.

The sun is on the other side of the building now and the temperature has cooled off nicely.

Another woman gets up to play a song by herself and says, "I'm going to do one by myself and then have the other people join me." The baglama player starts to play along with her, but the host pops up and runs over right away to stop him. I'm happy to see him do this.

He says, "Hey, you got to wait, man. She's doing this song by herself." Then she invites the djembe player to play with her, so it's a duo thing for one song. She definitely has a lot of confidence and is telling a story in between songs. Now she's inviting the bass player and the other people to come up to play along with her.

There are about 45 people in the back patio area at this point. I go inside and see another 25 people sitting in the air conditioning, having beer and food. This venue has beer and wine and a pretty extensive menu. The owners are a husband-and-wife team from St. Louis, and they do have a handful of St. Louis-themed things on the menu as well as décor nodding to that city.

It's 8:30 when we pay our bill and go our separate ways. We were drinking bottles of water and unsweetened iced tea all night. Rocky had a fried shrimp basket with cole slaw and fries. It is perfect timing, as some rain clouds have just moved in over the place.

The back patio has three fairly large tent roofs, so hopefully if it does start raining the musicians will be able to pack up safely. The wind has picked up and the temperature has dropped 5 to 10° — it's definitely a storm moving in. Collectively, we spent $35 in support of the event. Not a bad Monday night overall.

MONDAY, JUNE 5TH, 2023

We have returned to this venue for another open mic event because they have multiple hosts and we want to see what differences there might be in equipment, approach, etc. Are there going to be different musicians or will the same people be here? Maybe there will be a mix of new faces and regulars.

Rocky picks me up at 4:45 to head back down to the Pesky Pelican. We're trying to go to this open mic three times because they have three different hosts. One host does first and third Mondays, the second host does second Mondays, and the third host does fourth or last Mondays.

The open mic is from six to nine, and we arrive at 5:38, grabbing a seat at a small table as far away from the stage as possible. We were right up front last time and it became too loud for us. The fans are already on, but it's about 90° outside . There are rain clouds around, but we have a little shade under one of the tent roofs.

The host is setting up two mics on stands, a full drum set, and there are two wedge monitors on the ground. I can't see the brand name of the monitors. There are two line array towers with the subs in the back and middle of the stage area. It looks like a bass amp is also being provided. There's a 12- or 16-channel mixer in front of the stick towers.

Rocky asks our host about the two line arrays being right next to each other in the center of the back of the stage. He says that he likes to have them on opposite ends, that they provide a really good stereo sound, but because there's a high chance of rain today he has consolidated them in the middle to give him a better chance of protecting his equipment from getting rained on.

At 6:05 our host turns on some music. I think everything is set up, so maybe he's just making a few final preparations before playing a few songs. Rocky's next on the list. I don't see any other guitars here yet.

Rocky signed up first and as far as I can tell there are two other people on the list. We were here two weeks ago, but they didn't have an open mic on Memorial Day — the restaurant was closed.

The guy that played bass guitar when we were here two weeks ago walks in with his bass guitar in a backpack-style travel case.

It's 6:25 and our host is going to start this off by playing guitar and singing. The bass player just plugged in and another guy is sitting in on the drum set. Now it's a little bit of a sound check and I guess they are going to play some songs as a trio.

A woman who was here two weeks ago shows up with her guitar case. The woman with the djembe drum arrives and is getting set up off to the side, by the drummer. By the third song, the djembe drummer jumps into the jam. Our host announces that he's going to do one more song and then Rocky will get up and play.

It has cooled off a little bit because the sun is behind some big rain clouds at the moment. Our host is getting Rocky plugged in and set up on a stool. There are not as many people here as two weeks ago, but there are twenty-two people on the patio. In the middle of Rocky's first song, there's some high-pitched feedback and our host rushes to the mixer to make an adjustment.

During Rocky's third song, the sun comes out from behind the clouds and it is bearing down on me. I figure I've got a good twenty or thirty minutes before it gets behind the building.

Another guy shows up with a guitar case and signs in. I recognize him from an open mic the previous Thursday at Kahunas in St. Pete. The host comes over to the table next to mine to tell the next act to get ready, and explains that sometimes they do three songs per person but there are not a lot of names on the list right now so he's letting people do four or five songs each to fill the time. He tells Rocky to do one more, which will be his fourth.

I can see out to the parking lot where an SUV is being unloaded. Two women and two men emerge from the vehicle and the men are both carrying guitar cases. One of them is wearing a Beatles T-shirt. I'm going to assume they are probably a duo of some kind, but I am not sure.

The djembe player walks up in the middle of Rocky's last song and starts playing along. I hope that's okay with him, because I'm pretty sure she didn't ask first, which is an example of what I would consider bad etiquette. I make a mental note that the host didn't stop her or interject at all. So although this is advertised as an open mic, I guess it's really an open jam, which is not what I am looking for.

The next act is a solo musician, and it looks like the djembe player is joining him too. Our waitress comes to talk to me about ordering some food, so I don't actually notice if there is any communication between the djembe player and the guitar player.

At the same time, one of the women from the SUV has just brought in an electric guitar case, and the other woman has a very interesting telescope mic stand of a type I've never seen before. I'm not sure if she's playing an instrument or just helping put together the stand. At first, I thought it was some kind of camera stand. Now our host has joined in on the drum set to play with the djembe and guitar players.

When Rocky gets back to the table we order some food, and I ask him if it was okay with him that the woman who plays the djembe started jamming along with him on his last song. He tells me that he actually knows her from another jam he went to the day before and that it was totally cool — they had become friends and she can jam with him anytime if she wants to. I only knew her from when we were here two weeks ago and thought that it was weird for a complete stranger to just walk up and start playing with someone without asking for permission. I guess I was wrong.

It's 7:00 and now there are 32 people on the patio; things have picked up a little bit.

Our host isn't doing any introductions or saying things like "Put your hands together for so-and-so..." He is just calling out each name on the list from his table away from the microphones. Now the woman with her acoustic guitar is up there. The bass player and the djembe player are going to join her, with our host on drums.

Another man shows up and sits down at the host table where the list is. He's not carrying a guitar case but he does have the words "drummers wanted" on the back of his T-shirt, so I wonder if he's a drummer who's going to sit in with someone to jam. The woman named Raven who was here two weeks ago has also arrived.

The woman with the telescoping mic stand has attached an iPad holder clip and has a pad in front of her. It makes me think maybe she's a singer who doesn't play an instrument.

The guy with the "drummers wanted" T-shirt takes over on drums, and another guy asks the host if he can also play drums at some point.

Mark Hanson arrives. I had texted him earlier and told him we'd be here if he wanted to hang out. It's almost 7:30 and the sun is once again behind some clouds and almost down behind the building, so it's cooling off quite a bit.

A man shows up with a type of around-the-neck harmonica holder I'm not familiar with. Rocky talks to him and finds out it's a Hohner accessory and that he's had it for thirty-five years. I doubt they make them like that anymore, because in between talking to Mark I do a search and can't find any like it.

Now our host is singing on the second microphone — both are wireless, something I just noticed. So we have five people on stage now: a singer, a guitar player who sings, a bassist, a djembe player, and a drummer.

The next performer is a solo acoustic musician we saw at Kahuna's. On his second song, the djembe player joins in. Once again, I don't know if she asked or not. He ends up playing four songs.

The host is doing a little mixing and sound check for the woman with the pad and the telescope mic stand. She is going to sing backed by an electric guitarist, the bass guitarist, the djembe player, and a drummer. It is another five-person jam. While they are playing I notice that the guy with the harmonica around his neck has gone to his car and come back with an acoustic guitar in a hard case.

I'm trying to keep up with what's going on but I'm also having a lot of fun catching up with Mark.

He brings up a good point about people sticking around after they play their songs, and I realize that one of the previous acts has already left. Rocky had actually moved to his table and was talking to him for a little while. But the guy did hang out for a little while, probably half an hour, after he played.

Even if I wasn't "undercover" right now, I would still hang out. That's another reason why we arrived early — to get Rocky in one of the first spots on the list. Then we can hang out for another hour or two before we leave.

Rocky has the fish and chips this time and says he really likes it better than the shrimp. I have an order of fries because I need a light snack. We are both drinking unsweetened iced teas.

Raven, the percussionist, has joined the jam, playing a shaker and tambourine for one song. Then a new drummer gets behind the kit for a four-piece jam. They are doing one more song with the electric guitar player singing. Our host is now playing bass and the newest drummer is our third of the evening.

I'm glad we got a table at the back. It's not too loud back here but at this point, it is hard to carry on a conversation.

Another guy arrives carrying an acoustic guitar without a case and Rocky points him out as somebody who was at the open mic we went to at All Five Elements metaphysical shop the previous Saturday.

The woman with the electric guitar is joining the guy with the electric guitar for some songs as a duo. Our host joins them on drums.

At 8:30 we decide to head home. It was an interesting series of jams, but I hope when we come back next Monday to experience the third host it will be more solo acoustic musician performers.

Almost everybody who walked in with a guitar was approached by the bass player; I'm assuming he was asking if he could jam out with them. He doesn't know I play guitar, so he walks right past me each time. I know the host works a lot around my county. I met him one time when we both showed up to play a gig that was double-booked. But as far as I can tell, he didn't remember me and has no idea who I am.

MONDAY, JUNE 12TH, 2023

Today is our third and final visit to the Pesky Pelican open mic. Rocky picks me up at 5:15 and we arrive at 6:00. We meet our host in the parking lot; his name is Steve. When we arrive he is unloading his car and debating whether to go inside or not, because it is very hot today, with no rain clouds overhead.

It looks like he's going to set up outside, so I guess we're going to start at 6:30 which I wasn't sure about. Rocky looked it up online and it does say 6:30 on their website. I thought it started at 6:00, and the first two times we were here I may have believed things were starting late when in fact the host may have started early or on time.

It's ten after six, and our first musician has just walked in with a guitar case. There's nobody else on the patio but us, the host, and this new guy.

Steve is using a notebook for the sign-up list, and the same table the other two hosts have used. The PA is a Fishman stick line array-style speaker on a stand and what I believe is an 8-channel mixer sits next to that. He has a stool on the stage if somebody wants to sit, and there's one microphone on a stand.

The guitar player sits at the table next to us and begins chatting with Rocky about music stuff and sharing stories.

The woman with the djembe is here again, and another guy with a backpack guitar case has just come in and is talking to our host. I'm sure he will sign up. Our host is running some cables and places what I believe is a tuner pedal on the ground by the mic stand.

Our host is another local solo acoustic musician who plays gigs for a living. Many years ago, when I used to host an open mic night event, he would come around every now and then. We actually saw him at MacArthur's when we were there, and I didn't think he recognized me.

While I picked out our table, Rocky was over by the stage talking to him for a little while. He tells me that Steve had bought the first and third books in this series. I didn't think he'd recognized me, but I guess he did, so that's cool. I hope he doesn't try to get me up there to play, because I didn't bring my guitar with me. I just want to observe.

We get a table in the back of the venue, in the shade, and Rocky orders the fish and chips again.

The music cuts off and our host comes from inside the building. He is going to start off the show. Another musician has just taken his guitar case out of his car trunk and has a music stand with him, too. He has grabbed a table and now there are also a couple of people that are just customers. A woman who's been here the two previous times we came also just arrives with her guitar case. It is nice that everybody seems to know each other and offers little waves or nods to say hello.

Our host is about to start playing and the djembe player is at her station by her drum. It looks like one of the other guitar players, a young guy with a cutaway acoustic, is also going to play. After the first song, our host makes some announcements about the event.

It's been a hot day and it's still 86 degrees. I am very happy we were able to get a table in the shade and the venue has cranked up all the fans around the patio, so there's a little bit of air moving.

I don't think I've ever heard one of these Fishman stick PA systems in person and it sounds really good. The lead guitar is crisp, and the rhythm guitar is full, while the djembe player is miked up again. We can hear and understand the vocals and everything that's plugged into the mixer. I'm actually impressed by the sound system tonight. I look it up: a Fishman SA220 Solo Performance System.

I watch a guy ride a bicycle across the back of the parking lot with a guitar — but no case — strapped to his back. I assume he is coming to the open mic.

In the middle of the third song our host breaks a string; I think they were going to do one or two more songs, too. Rocky is headed to the stage a little bit earlier than expected. He has his guitar out of the case and tuned up already. Our host makes sure to tell everybody to clap for the lead guitar player, whom he says he met just this past Thursday, and also for the djembe player. There's not a lot of us here, but everybody claps.

Rocky has become friends with Melanie the djembe player and they're chatting, so I think she's going to stay there on the stage and jam along with him. I wonder what songs Rocky will pick out tonight.

I was right; the guy who rode his bike here with his guitar strapped to his back comes to the patio area, grabs a table and places his guitar on a chair.

Rocky is singing a song he wrote about our host, Steve. They have been friends for many years so that's pretty cool. A couple of other guys with no instruments have arrived and they're talking to Steve. One guy has a shirt that says More Cowbell. That's funny. Maybe he's a percussionist or drummer — maybe we could get lucky and he brought a cowbell, which would be awesome!

Rocky does four songs and now the guy at the table next to us is getting up to play. He has a Taylor GS mini guitar. Melanie is going to play her djembe with him as well. When we were talking to him, he mentioned that he only plays original songs, so I am very interested to hear his set.

The bass player guy from the last two times we were here wheels a cart with a big bass amp in it around the building, and has his backpack guitar case. He's off to the side of the stage at the moment, but that lets us know that there's going to be some kind of jam happening and that he's going to join in at some point.

During our second act's fourth and final song, a man and a woman walk onto the patio from inside the restaurant carrying guitar cases. I don't like to assume, but maybe they are a duo that plays songs together. I notice something like half a sock on the microphone. The guy after Rocky plays his originals, takes it off the microphone, and he's done with his set.

The next performer is the young gentleman who played lead along with our host for the first three songs of the night. He's going to be playing and singing some songs, and Melanie stays at her drum and plays with him as well. They're playing a blues song when the guy with the More Cowbell shirt walks up with two bongos on a stand and starts jamming along with them. The guitar player has a red pedal I couldn't identify when he set up. He just built a loop over the chord progression and now he's playing some lead guitar over the loop.

Another guitar player has pulled a chair up to the front of the stage and is trying to play along. The main performer invites him to plug into the PA and jam. Now we have two guitar players, a djembe player, and the bongo player, who went somewhere else then came back. They play four songs together. Our host comes over to talk and I learn that the lead guitar player is a guitar teacher at one of our local music stores.

Another woman with a Taylor GS Mini guitar case has showed up on the porch. It's finally cooling down a little bit and more people are arriving to hang out. Our next performer is playing a very interesting-looking guitar and I'm going to have to ask him about it. It comes together in pieces, and he has asked the other two guitar players to stay on stage and join him.

I go to the bathroom and when I return, the lead guitar player is soloing while the other guitar player has moved over to Melanie's djembe drum. They are playing a Beatles song.

The interesting-looking guitar has a lot of fuzz, and they're discussing what the problem might be — it might be the battery, or maybe something's wrong with the guitar or the cable. The host is helping him investigate, because it is making some very strange noises. The guy says it's brand-new, so maybe it's something to do with the battery pack.

The other guitar player who switched to djembe has offered to let him use his guitar and he has accepted. They switch by unplugging his guitar and plugging him into the other guy's. They do another cover song and then the guy singing announces that they're going to play one of his original songs. He has one of those see-through music stands with some papers clipped onto it so they won't fall or fly away.

When I was inside the air conditioning felt nice, and I did go to the dining room to see if anybody was there, but there weren't any extra people.

After his last song, the guy jokes that he paid everybody five bucks to clap. Next up is the woman who's been here every time we've been here so far, and wanted to play solo the first week before bringing other players up to jam. Tonight, she announces this into the microphone and says, "Only when I say by myself alone on my own, that also means with Melanie on the drum thing."

True to her word, she calls the bass player and the lead guitar player up, and even invites one of the other guitar players. He says he wants to listen and chill. So now we have a four-piece onstage. Once again, she is very confident on the microphone and talks to the crowd between songs.

It seems excessively hot tonight — I am sweating. I order a side of fries and I also do something I normally wouldn't and order a cold beer.

The singer's doing an original parody of a song. I don't know what it is, but it's a very popular song and she's playing the chords and using the melody. In the lyrics, she's talking about how the people that play here get one free beer. I never knew that. No one ever told us we get one free beer if we get up and play.

The group were going to do one more song, but our host steps in to stop them after three. I hear him say there are six more people on the list and it's 8:00, so he's trying to move down the list and get people up to play. It's good to see him being attentive to the situation.

Our next performer includes our lead guitar player and they both put capos on the third fret of their instruments. The bass player and the djembe player are in on the jam as well; the bongo player is on tambourine and our previous performer is singing backup harmonies on an extra microphone. Something seems familiar about the guy who's singing lead, and Rocky tells me he was an act at the metaphysical store open mic night.

The guy at the bongos has switched from tambourine to using some drumsticks on the bongos.

Another player has shown up that we saw the previous Friday night. A few other customers are hanging out and getting food and drinks, which fills out the audience. It is now 8:19 and we're going to leave in about ten minutes, at 8:30. Believe it or not, the jam is getting quite loud.

The next act is the male-female guitar duo, and they're discussing something with Melanie at the djembe, so we'll see if she jams with them or not. Each of them carried a guitar case into the event, but it turns out the woman is just going to sing, and not play. The man's going to play his guitar and use a microphone on the mic stand and Melanie will join them.

For the first time tonight, there are some feedback problems as the duo are soundchecking. It's the female singer's microphone and they get it figured out, but Rocky and I split to head home. I think this has been my favorite experience at this venue for Monday open mic nights.

NORTH END TAPHOUSE

Rocky picks me up at 4:15 and we drive south for an hour to the town of Gulfport. We get to the North End Tap House and Kitchen in what they call the Village Courtyard at about 5:15 for tonight's open mic. They have a nice stage with a mural behind it, and we notice a guy bringing speakers to the stage. I'm guessing this is our host for the evening and we are the first people to arrive.

While we are waiting around I am checking out the area and I notice a mural of John Prine painted on the wall. I go over and read the words and look closer at the picture. I have heard that he used to have a house in Gulfport, and this mural of him confirms it for me. He passed away a couple of years ago now. People in the area used to ask me to play one of his songs, and I did finally learn "Let's Talk Dirty In Hawaiian," which is a cute, funny "play on words" type of song.

As the host is setting up, I'm looking at the equipment; it looks like he's setting up a 12 or 16-channel mixer on the side of the stage. He's got a few mic stands and a couple of Alto speakers on stands. They are 12s with horns, and two QSC monitors that are 15s with horns.

Rocky asks him about signing up on the list and finds out his name is Gabe. He says he will bring the list over when he's done setting up.

Rocky signs up first and another guy shows up with a guitar case and gets signed up as well. When Gabe was at our table talking to us, I told him that he looked familiar, and he said he is the owner of a music school and concert venue in St. Petersburg called Noisemakers.

Mark Hanson arrives and a couple more guitar players show up with their instruments as well. We are talking about an interesting thing I'd never seen before — a classical guitar strap. Rocky has brought a classical guitar tonight and when he puts on the strap I ask him about it. Evidently, it's the same kind of strap Willie Nelson uses when he plays his famous guitar, Trigger. I laugh at this because I had always wondered, "What is that little belt on Willie Nelson's guitar?" I thought it was something that was holding his guitar together, because is so beaten up that I guessed it was like a little belt keeping the wood from splitting, but evidently it's a classical guitar strap. I didn't realize classical guitars don't come with a strap button — the little piece of metal that the strap grips at each end. On most acoustic-electric guitars this would also be the input jack for your cable on the bottom of your guitar.

It is now 6:00 and Leify Green has shown up. I thought he was typically the host, but Gabe told me they were co-hosting tonight. Gabe is putting on his guitar and about to start the open mic when a loud rumble of thunder is heard. There are some big clouds in the distance, and I hope they stay over there.

We are outside under a big tent and the stage has a covered roof. The last time I was here there was no tent, and they rearranged the tables. Hopefully the storm will go around us. It is not on top of us at the moment; it's a beautiful, hot sunny day.

Gabe's doing a little sound check on the mics now and announcing that this is an open mic and industry night. I think this means people in the restaurant and music industry will get some kind of discount.

It's only ten after six — it's still pretty early, but there are already six guys with guitars here, and a few tables where non-musicians are having food and beers. Leify Green brings out two more speakers to set up — Mackie 12s with horns.

Gabe asks everybody to please make a nice round of applause for Rocky, and the thunder rumbles again in the distance. Everybody stops for a second and looks up.

In between musicians, they have to switch out a couple of cables and I see a classical guitar capo sitting on our table. It has a unique way of coming on and off the fretboard that you can do with one hand very quickly. When Rocky gets back to the table, he explains it to us and I do a quick web search because I have never seen anything quite like it before.

"The Fender Smart Capo is lightweight and easy to use. The Classical Model can be moved with one hand for quick changes while performing. The special design produces perfect tension across all strings, eliminating string buzz while keeping strings in tune."

That is two accessories today that I've never seen before.

The next act is a duo of sorts. A man is playing an acoustic with his fingers and another man is going to join him on the harmonica. The guitar player is going to play what he announces are original political satire songs that he has been writing, and that he thinks are funny to hopefully make people laugh. This should be different.

Both hosts are trying to fix a problem and we're not sure what's happening, but they have switched out a couple of speakers and run some different cables. Clearly, there's a technical difficulty happening with the PA system. We can still hear the music because it's coming out of some of the speakers, but not all. What has happened is that one of the tweeters is blown in one of the Altos speakers. The area we're in has multiple restaurants and one of them owns the Mackie speakers. The hosts are trying to figure out if they can maybe use those speakers. They are hoping to have a house system of some kind here in the future, so that the hosts don't always have to bring their own stuff and everybody helps each other in collaboration on this sound system.

There are over 50 people now in the common courtyard that is shared by, I think, three restaurants.

A lady who just got up to sing says she's been on a 12-year hiatus from performing, that she has stage fright and she's very nervous. She's not playing an instrument — she is holding her phone speaker up to one of the microphones while she sings on another. Believe it or not, the music is loud enough for this to work. I've never seen anyone do this before, so this is quite a unique experience. Mark leans in and says, "When she's done we are going to give her a standing ovation." She actually does really well — to this point, each act has performed four songs, but she has prepared two.

The next act of the evening is a colorful fellow with a classical guitar covered in stickers. I've been told by some other people he has an auto-wah on his guitar at all times, so I'm looking forward to hearing that. Everything he does is very percussive; he slaps the thumb of his picking hand against the top corner of the guitar. He is playing without a pick, but not finger-picking. Is a very interesting sound. He plays three songs and everybody claps.

I found out later that he had a Tonewood amp on the back of his guitar. That was how he was getting the auto-wah effect. I saw the wire running to the amp, but I didn't put two and two together the first time I saw him play.

Now one of our hosts is tuning up a violin and making some announcements. He builds up a percussive type of loop by tapping on the body of the violin and adding some lower chordal-type things. Now he's playing a beautiful lead over the top. This is quite an eclectic group of musicians with different moods and feelings. After this beautiful instrumental piece, he invites a little girl up — one of his two daughters. She has a really little violin and I think they're going to do a song together. And now he is playing an Emerald carbon-fiber guitar from Ireland. So we have an acoustic-electric finger-picking with a little girl that's going to play violin over it. It's a very pretty song, and he's singing while his daughter is playing violin. (I haven't heard the thunder for a while and the sun is coming through the trees.) He creates a loop with the guitar chord progression and while his daughter is playing her part, he begins playing lead violin over the top. It's quite beautiful.

Right in the middle of this beautiful song, a guy walks up on the stage and starts setting up a bass guitar and an amp. I have to say, that's very rude and bad etiquette on his part. I think he should have waited and done this in between songs or between acts, but apparently they know each other and everyone is okay with it. It is a casual atmosphere and a laid-back scene.

The host makes an announcement about the event's sponsors, which include the various restaurants, the music school, and a local radio station.

The next act is a solo musician with an acoustic guitar who asks the bass player and the violin player to join him for a trio jam of some kind on what he says is his original music. It seems that people are being limited to two, three or four songs, rather than a certain span of time. The last time I was here was the previous October, and they were using a ten-minute time limit then.

We are drinking water and iced tea, and Rocky gets a hot Italian sandwich which he says is awesome. I have to admit it looks delicious, especially the bread. Around 8:30, we decide to head home. The weather stayed beautiful, and it was a fun time.

TUESDAY, MAY 30TH, 2023

Rocky has come by my house at 4:15 to pick me up. We're headed back to North End Tap House for a second time, to see who the host is this week and see if some different people come out to play, along with some of the same people who were there last week.

I met Rocky more than ten years ago, when I was hosting an open mic at a tap house in Palm Harbor that had craft beer and wine. We have been friends ever since, and it's been a lot of fun hanging out and spending time together while working on this project. Rocky is 74 years old and has been playing guitar for a long time. He has written a few songs that in my opinion are pretty creative. He also plays some cover songs. He is a Florida native who graduated from the University of Florida back in 1970.

We roll into the North End Tavern about twenty after five, and we aren't the first ones there. A few other musicians are hanging out already. I'm looking at the John Prine mural again. This is what it says...

"In a town this size, there's no place to hide.
Everywhere you go you meet someone you know.
You can't steal a kiss in a place like this.
How the rumors do fly in a town this size,
in a town this size, in a town this size."
—John Prine

These are lyrics from one of his songs. It sure does add a special touch to the mural. It makes sense because he owned a house here in Gulfport and it is a small town.

While we wait for other people to show up, I walk across the street to a bar/restaurant that is under new ownership and has changed its name. I meet the general manager and give him my card. They do not have live music yet and we discuss the possibility of starting a music program. He will check out my promo video and we'll talk again later.

Leify Green is our host this week. He arrives at about 5:40 and puts out the list. Seven or eight people swarm it like bees. I see a bass player has brought an amp to the stage and our host is rolling in a cart full of guitars, amps, and speakers. Some other people have gone to get their guitars.

Rocky signed up in the fifth slot this time. One new thing this week is that there is a door on the stage leading to a storage area; our host is pulling out the Mackie speakers that were used last week when there was a problem with the Alto speakers. Maybe they are moving forward with a house PA system, or at least a subsidized version with the speakers from the restaurant next door.

The bass player from last week is here now and that means we have two bassists available to jam with people. At least the guy from last week is here earlier than last time and won't interrupt anybody by setting up.

Three other people have shown up to play and are on the list now. This gives us eleven acts. It's starting off pretty well and looks like it'll be a pretty good turnout. When our host put out the list, he said there were 12 guaranteed spots. I'm not sure if there's a time limit or a maximum number of songs, but I guess we'll find out as we go.

Our host is almost done setting up the P.A. and it's ten after six. He is very fast at setting up, and it seems like a relaxed atmosphere.

It's 6:15 when our first act takes the stage — a duo with an acoustic-electric Taylor guitar and the new bass player, who has just introduced himself to everybody. Our host makes the announcement that the open mic is getting started, and they do some mic checks.

The first duo plays three songs in 15 minutes. Our host makes some announcements about future events. In June, they're going to start at 7:00 instead of 6:00 because in summer the days are longer. Sign-ups will start at 6:30.

During the switch, the bass player from the first act packed up his bass and amp. I guess he was just playing those few songs with his friend. I had assumed he would make himself available for jamming with others, but I am pleasantly surprised that he is not, because the jams tend to get a lot louder than the solo and duo acts.

Our next performer is a solo acoustic musician playing an Epiphone guitar. He started off with an original song. During his second original, another new guitar player showed up and signed up on the list.

While our next act is setting up his pedal board and getting his guitar out of the case, our host makes some announcements about sponsors and everybody claps.

Our host puts on some music through the speakers while our next act gets ready to play. He has grabbed a bar stool from somewhere in the courtyard, and is using his own microphone. That's something I would do as well because I don't want to catch anybody else's germs and I like my microphone. But he adjusts the microphone stand without tightening it, and in the middle of the first verse of his first song, it begins to slowly sink down. Eventually, our host sees what is going on and jumps onstage to tighten it up for him. There are more problems; his guitar starts to lose volume and the host gives him a different cable to run from his guitar to his pedal board. It works! Now he has looped a chord progression and is playing some lead over it and things seem to be going well. It was good to see the host help figure out the technical difficulties. The guy was playing a rather expensive Taylor guitar and it was weird to hear it lose signal that way.

There are three or four musicians who were here last week, and other than that it's all new faces. The whole courtyard has more than 50 people in it now, including patrons who are just here to have food and drinks while listening to the music, which is awesome.

Our host says, "Make some noise and give a big round of applause for (insert name)," then turns on some music because the guy needs a little extra breakdown time to switch out his mic and pack up his pedal board.

The next act has an acoustic guitar and a very fancy rack around his neck holding a rather large harmonica. I do a little search and see that it's a chromatic harmonica. We think his guitar is an Alvarez brand. I guess I would label him a folk musician. He starts off with some harmonica over the acoustic, playing a nice song about traveling and working on the railroad. He's playing original songs that are pretty cool. Our host announced that the format is three songs or 15 minutes, whichever comes first, but this guy's songs are very short so he gives him a fourth song because he was still under ten minutes.

The chromatic harmonica is a type of harmonica that uses a button-activated sliding bar to redirect air from the hole in the mouthpiece to the selected reed plate desired. When the button is not pressed, an altered diatonic major scale of the key of the harmonica is available, while depressing the button accesses the same scale a semitone higher in each hole. Thus, the instrument is capable of playing the 12 notes of the Western chromatic scale. The chromatic harmonica can thus be contrasted with a standard harmonica, which can play only the notes in a given musical key.

Rocky orders a sandwich and is told that since he's playing, he gets 20% off of his food and drinks. I think that's the industry night part of this event.

The last time we were here, there was no table service; we had to go inside to order from the bar. But this week they have help at the bar and the employees are tending to the crowd and doing table service.

Rocky is up next. He surprises me by playing a couple of songs that he wrote about other people that go to the open mics, which I had never heard before.

Following Rocky is the guy from the previous week with the Tonewood amp. He wears very colorful clothes, and his guitar is covered in stickers.

The next act moves one of the two microphone stands to the middle of the stage, brings up a stool, and sits down to play guitar and sing. He's going to be playing a finger-picking style. He starts with an old blues song from back in the 1950s, followed by one from the '60s and another from the '50s.

It's a quarter to eight now and it has cooled off a lot, as the sun is almost down behind the building. The crowd in the courtyard has grown to more than seventy people. It's pretty busy, and it's a beautiful evening.

The next performer is the solo acoustic musician who was here last week joined by the bass player and violin player. This week he is playing alone.

The next person who takes the stage is playing accordion. I think it's going to plug in just like a guitar on a quarter-inch cable. We were going to leave at 8:30, but we wanted to wait to see this guy. The host had him plugged in, but the cord fell out or something, so they moved the other mic over and so now it's miked up. He is quite a character — it has been acoustic guitars all night, so we are getting a real treat with the very rare appearance of an accordion.

Our host announces that the next act is the last one on the list, and then he's going to play. He's a solo acoustic musician playing a Takamine. Rocky leans over and tells me that this is the host of the open mic where we are going the next night.

We leave about ten minutes before nine. Some of the other musicians had already left, too, and the crowd had thinned a little bit. It was pretty busy during the middle part of the event and a lot of the musicians did stick around after they played; I don't think anyone played and then just left right after their songs.

It was a nice experience and it seems to be a pretty well-run open mic night event with a casual and loose format. Coupled with the industry night discount it's pretty cool.

TUESDAY, JUNE 6TH, 2023

We are headed back down to the North End Tap House. Rocky is bringing his wife Sue and her Celtic harp with him this time and we are going to get there around 6:30 since the start time is now 7:00. Along the way we're going to stop off at a restaurant with a tiki bar attached to a seafood market. I have messaged them about playing there through a social media app.

The owner reached out to me and asked me to stop by sometime and meet him in person. It is on the way, so we've allotted me a few minutes to pop in there to give him my card, shake his hand, and talk briefly. Then we will get to the open mic and get Rocky and Sue signed up on the list and settle in for an evening of music, food, and iced tea.

We arrive at 6:30 and Rocky signs up on the list right away. We have two hosts this week and their names are Cameron and

Levi. They have a couple of EV speakers set up. One of them is on a stand and one is actually next to the building, across the patio on the other side of the tables. It looks like there's one monitor on the stage, two mic stands, two mics, and a music stand. There is a Boss brand multi-effects pedal board on the stage that the hosts are going to use for an electric guitar that is going through the PA rather than a guitar amp.

The hosts suggest getting Sue's Celtic harp and chair set up on the stage so that she doesn't have to carry it up when it's their turn. I would imagine they're first or second on the list, because only one other open-mic musician is here at this point. We've seen him at both of the last two events.

The later start was a great idea, because the sun is already on the other side of the main building. It's cooler here than it has been any of the other times we've been here, and they have their fans on, moving the air around a little bit.

What looks like a 12-channel mixer sits on a little table at the side of the stage. It's about 10 minutes before the event is due to start and our co-hosts are warming up by playing softly together, one on acoustic guitar and the other on electric.

Cameron, one of the hosts, begins making announcements about the sponsoring companies, and explaining that they're going to give each act 10 to 12 minutes onstage. Cameron is playing a Stratocaster and Levi's playing a Martin acoustic.

During their first song, a woman comes in and signs up on the list. I can't see if she has a guitar case with her or not.

After their third song, our hosts switch guitars and now Cameron is on acoustic and Levi is on electric. Cameron is singing lead as Levi is playing lead guitar. It's cool to see a duo where each person can play lead guitar or sing lead vocals.

That's a little different from the normal duo format. They say this will be their last song and they'll start going down the list. Rocky and Sue are up next.

The hosts make kind of a big deal about having a unique instrument on stage, because the Celtic harp is not something you see very often. They also call them "our first presenters," which is a unique way of saying performer or act. In my mind, it means that the musician is presenting their music to the audience, the same way an artist is presenting their art.

On a side note, I get lucky because there is a brewery I've been trying to get into for a few years now, and the owner used to come to some of my open mics a long time ago. He's here and is going to sign up and play some songs. We chat a little bit about me playing at the brewery, which is great. You never know who will show up at the open mic! I make sure to get his cell number.

Hopefully, I'll get some gigs — his brewery is in a town called Safety Harbor, which is fifteen minutes from my house.

While we're talking, two more people show up with their guitar cases and sign onto the list. It's a little bit lighter turn-out for musicians and regular customers this week, but there's still about 30 people on the patio in the courtyard village.

Rocky and Sue sound really good tonight; I can tell that they have been practicing.

The musician that was here when we arrived has been here every time we've come to this open mic. That makes me think that he lives nearby and probably comes every week consistently. Other than that, I don't see any of the people from the previous two weeks. It's mostly new people.

When Rocky and Sue are done, one of the hosts calls up the brewery owner. He had just gone to his car and comes back down the passageway leading to the courtyard as they're calling him to the stage like he's a rockstar or something.

He has a harmonica around his neck and is playing folky-type music. He plays only original songs. He said to me there was nobody else on the list for a few spots, so he can go on now and then he's going to another local beach bar to hear a specific band that he likes that plays there every Tuesday night. He told me who is in the band, and they're all top-notch local musicians that get together and jam out on Tuesday nights. We do have a lot of good musicians in the Tampa Bay area, and quite a vibrant music scene as far as I'm concerned.

Mark Hanson arrives and joins our table. I'm sure we'll hear some fun stories and jokes since he's quite a fun character that likes to cut it up and make us all laugh.

Our hosts are doing a really good job with the sound. They're using EV 12s with horns, the same speakers I just bought, and everything sounds awesome.

Our friend the brewer does four beautiful original songs, playing finger-picking style on a Gibson acoustic.

Next we hear a duo of acoustic guitar players — the guy who was here the last two weeks, plus another person we didn't know playing some lead on his original songs. Then our hosts go back up, again taking turns switching back and forth from acoustic to electric and singing leads and harmonies. They're really good and it's really cool to see.

They spot somebody in the audience that they know plays guitar and ask him, "Did you bring a guitar?" He says no, so they gave him the host's acoustic guitar and one of them is going to play electric along with him. We have a new impromptu duo.

It's ten minutes to nine and there's nobody else on the list, which is why the host called out to his friend and gave him a guitar to use. It's been a lower turnout than the first two times we were here. It still is a lovely night, and the music has been really good, just not as busy as what we've come to think of as normal in this venue.

Rocky and I each had two bottles of unsweetened iced tea, and he had the hot Italian sandwich again. His wife, Sue, had a glass of white wine before they went on stage and another after they played. It is important to spend a little bit of money in support of the open mic event, so the venue can make money and be able to pay the host. We didn't spend a lot but as part of the community, we did our part.

BREWERS TASTING ROOM

THURSDAY, MAY 25TH, 2023
ST. PETERSBURG, FL

I was invited to this open mic by another local SAM a little over a month ago. I was told tonight would be the last open mic event at this location after a nine-year run, because the business is closing its doors. I have heard good things about the host, and that he has found a new location for the event starting next week. Everything starts at 6 PM and Rocky is going to pick me up at 4:30. We are going down to St. Petersburg again, but a different part of town than the last two open mics we have visited.

We arrive at the place at 5:35 and see the host setting up a drum set. He already has two mics set up on stands, with an iPad holder attached to one. There is one Alto brand speaker that looks like a 10" with a horn on a stand, and another of the same size as a monitor wedge on the floor.

The place is pretty busy with what looks like an after work young professionals and businesspeople crowd. Brewers is a tasting room or tap room for craft beer that also sells wine and has a kitchen with cheesesteaks, tacos, wings, and things like that. The kitchen is called Cheesesteak Company and they used to be a food truck until they settled here.

The place has a lot of the features of a normal tap room, and it looks like they might actually brew some beer here as well. There are chalkboard menus on the walls. It's located in a shopping center on the east side of St. Pete, near the Gandy Bridge that goes across to Tampa.

There is no waitstaff (at some point one person does show up to work the floor) so I go to the bar to get us some water and a menu. I ask the bartender if they brew beer here and he says they used to, hence the equipment.

Rocky signs up on the list and tells me that he'll be on at 6:30 and that the spots are 15 minutes apart.

There are just over 50 people inside, and more on the front and side patios. There are speakers on the patios which must have an XLR input for the host to plug into from the P.A system.

Another guy shows up with some cymbals and some attachments for the drum kit, along with a large speaker. He also carries in what looks like a pair of congas or djembe drums attached to some kind of stand. I don't know if this is a duo partner or co-host yet.

The host of the open mic is named Charles or Charlie. It is 6:10 and he has been tuning his guitar and getting ready to start for a few minutes now. He is using an iPad that has a mixer on it to run the sound. The drummer brings in a drum stool and sets it down next to the double percussion instrument stand.

Charlie starts playing a song at 6:15, but quickly stops and makes an announcement that anyone who is a musician should sign up on the list. Then he begins playing his first song for real.

Charlie's playing a beat-up old Gibson by himself, SAM style. He plays three songs in 10 minutes, and nobody's filled in the second spot on the list, so Rocky's up next. Four or five other people have come in and signed up to play, then shuffled off to the bar to grab a beer, hang out, and listen.

Charlie gives Rocky a loud introduction and everybody claps. A group of about eight people just came in, including a very young-looking girl carrying a guitar case.

Rocky ends up playing for 20 minutes, and now our host is making some announcements. He is very outgoing and confident on the microphone. The next act is another Solo Acoustic Musician playing an old Gibson guitar. They do a little bit of a soundcheck and the host is using a mixer on the iPad from out in front of the crowd. He has set up a little station for himself across the room from the stage, behind the end of the bar.

The venue is a rather large warehouse-type room in a strip mall shopping center-type building. It can be tough to get good sound in these types of rooms, but it is decent. A guy named Mike introduces himself to Rocky and they are chatting about songs and guitar music. The majority of the audience is just a normal bar crowd; they're talking and being kind of loud. It's quite a difference from the last two open mics we went to that were outside with most of the people listening and being quiet. Maybe there were more musicians and friends and family at those venues, whereas here there are more customers than musicians.

After three songs and 15 minutes, our host Charlie gets up and calls for everybody to give it up for the musician. Now he's presenting the next act, another solo acoustic musician. I have to admit I was worried when I got here and saw the drum set that this might be an open jam all night. But so far it's been all solo acoustic musicians. Mike, the guy who was talking to Rocky, is tuning up his guitar and has a metal harmonica holder around his neck so I think he might be up soon.

Back to back, we hear from a James Taylor/Jackson Browne type of musician, and someone who's more of a heavy metal type, playing fast eighth notes and wearing a lightning bolt guitar strap. It's very interesting to see all the different styles of musicians during these undercover trips to open mics. I had no real expectations coming in, so each person's musical style or unique instrument is a surprise. It is definitely making it fun for me as an audience member.

Mike, the guy who was talking to Rocky, gets a loud welcome. FYI, a metal harmonica holder is called "The Rack." You put your harmonica in it, hang it around your neck, and you can play both harmonica and guitar at the same time.

Mike plays a song called "Pirates From Tampa" and tells us that it was written by another local musician he knows. It is quite a spirited song, and if you don't know the history of Tampa Bay, this is a really good pirate song. When he finishes, the whole bar claps and cheers and whistles. He says, "That's it, I'm only doing that one song," and comes over and talks to us for a minute, sharing some information about another open mic on Wednesdays at an Irish bar down the street.

Now the young girl I saw earlier is getting up to play. She's performing solo too and she has a beautiful orange Gretsch electric guitar. She is really good and very confident on the microphone. She gets the most applause of the night so far. I don't know how to describe her performance, but it was very pop-rock and very cool. She had good dynamics, a beautiful voice, and played some surprisingly technical guitar lines. She's 18 years old and playing original songs.

And now we're on to our next act, another woman playing solo acoustic in more of a folk style. She only does two songs and says, "That's it for me," and it was very nice original music.

Our next act is going to be solo as well. He has a classical guitar and a small pedal board, and does a fairly upbeat song with vocals before going right into a beautiful classical guitar finger-picking style instrumental.

While he's playing, another fellow shows up with a rather large case that I assume contains a bass. He goes outside to talk with the drummer/percussionist. Now our performer is singing and fingerpicking, which is cool. I'm very impressed with the confidence of a lot of the players here. This guy tells a story about his next song, a cover of a song written by a Florida band from Brooksville, a town about an hour north of here.

I talk to Rocky about the major differences in the venues and locations we have been to so far, as well as the wide range of musicians. We are in the northern part of St. Petersburg, right by the highway to Tampa, and it's much more of a city style. Our first open mic was close to the beach and our second mic was in a little downtown area. Each spot has a totally different type of clientele and environment, that draws in different types of musicians.

I see somebody come in with a little rectangular case and put it behind the stage. He pulls out a mandolin and takes it outside to warm up. Our host welcomes our new player, a Solo Acoustic Musician playing a Takamine brand guitar. Evidently, he just moved to town. He's playing finger-style — his guitar doesn't have a pickguard, and it's definitely worn in that spot from lots of playing. His songs, which are originals, are really pretty, and he has a nice voice, but I can't understand the words.

We find out about another open mic on Sundays, and we're going to try to go to one of those sometime soon. There has been a little bit of networking tonight and it has been a little tougher to stay undercover. It got so busy we had a few different people join us at our table. We had four chairs and there were only two of us, so we shared some space and it helped us get a lead on this other open mic which happens to be very near my house. I didn't even know about it.

The guy that just played is now being joined by his uncle as a duo. The uncle is doing a song about Captain Morgan and rum which is very appropriate for Tampa Bay. His nephew is using a pick now and playing lead guitar.

Around 8:30, we decide to leave. We had driven through a storm to get here, and there's a big storm over us as we leave the parking lot. The music was getting louder and louder and there was going to be a drum set and bass involved very soon, so that was enough for me for the night. As we were driving home, we were talking about the differences in the open mics so far. Things like how tonight's host was using a pad to mix the PA while standing behind the bar, which we thought was kind of cool. Rocky commented to me that there were 26 people signed up on the list. I think that is the most we've seen so far.

MCARTHURS IRISH PUB

WEDNESDAY, MAY 31ST, 2023
ST. PETERSBURG, FL

When we were at the Brewer's Tasting Room open mic, we met some other musicians and were made aware of this Wednesday night event. McArthurs Irish Pub is on the same street and just down the road, on the opposite side of the highway from where we were last week. The open mic starts at 7 PM and has a featured performer, a new aspect that we haven't encountered so far on our journey.

When we walk in it's very dark and there are a lot of traditional Irish things on the walls. There is a nice wooden bar with tall chairs and we grab a high-top table that has a reserved sign on it. It requires five people to be seated there, so we ask another open mic player and his wife to join us.

His name is Overdue Bill; I met him once when I was playing at Harbor Master Tiki, which I discussed in SAM 3, and I gave him a sticker that night. He's a local musician and he'll be the featured performer of the night. I thought he would play during the final hour, but he's going to go on stage in the middle of the event.

There is a stage on the left as you walk in through the front door. Our host is named Steady Eddie — we met him last week at the Brewers Tasting Room open mic. He was also in the audience and signed up to play the previous night in Gulfport.

There are two 12" QSC speakers with horns on speaker stands bolted to the wall; I assume they are house speakers, and Eddie has what looks like a 12-channel mixer on the table to the back of the stage, with a couple of mics set up on stands. There is a Samson brand speaker right in front of the stage on a box, serving as a monitor for the performers.

We can see the stage from our table, but we're far enough away that I hope it won't be too loud. Rocky picked me up at 5:30 and we got here right at 6:30; the open mic starts at 7:00. He brought his wife and her Celtic harp.

Our host comes to the table to get everybody signed up on the list and we find out that Overdue Bill will go on around 8:30.

The menu has lots of traditional Irish food like corned beef and cabbage, Scotch eggs, and those kinds of things.

Mike, who does the "Pirates of Tampa" song, arrives and signs up. I hope he does that song tonight because it was super fun and full of energy. He's the person who told us about this place at the Brewers Tasting Room's open mic.

My cover is not blown, but Overdue Bill is currently reading the second book and I did give him a sticker when I met him. He knows who I am but he doesn't know I am doing research for this book. I didn't know he had bought the first and second books and he's talking to me about things in them, which is fun.

I notice two other people that were at Brewers Tasting Room last week. We have six chairs at our table and Mike has joined us. This makes for a fun time and lots of conversation.

Bill orders a Guinness stew and his wife gets a Reuben sandwich — the food looks awesome. The place is really cool. There are only two TVs in the bar area and it's not a sports bar. It's actually an authentic Irish atmosphere and menu. I can't believe I've never been here before.

We find out about another open mic on Tuesdays, and I am sure we will make our way there soon. Meeting new people and networking with other musicians is a big part of going to open mic events. There is a group of people who enjoy the camaraderie and community fellowship that they experience when sharing time and space with other musicians.

Promptly at 7:00, our host takes to the stage. The waitress delivers some food for Mike. He ordered the chicken pot pie, and it looks delicious. I'm going to have to come back to this place for dinner sometime. Our host says he'll be mixing up originals and a few cover songs, and his set goes quite well.

Rocky and Sue are up next, and they are getting her Celtic harp set up. The host helps them get situated on the stage. Her harp has twenty-nine strings and it sounds beautiful.

They told me they picked out three songs, with an extra one as well just in case they are asked to do four. I see that our host is using an iPad to mix the sound from the passageway between the bar room and the dining room, which is right in front of our table and straight ahead to the stage. It is a pretty good spot to mix from.

Our next act is a duo — a blind man playing an Ovation acoustic/electric guitar and a woman who will sing along with him. Her harmonies fill the sound out wonderfully. They have a stage name of "Paper and Strings," and I am told it's because he is the strings, because he plays guitar, and she is the paper because she reads the words from her songbook, which is now on a pad. They started with a cover song but follow that with an original song. Bill points out that the guitarist puts a baby sock over the microphone when he sings as a preventative measure against the spread of germs. It reminded me of someone else who I saw do the same thing at the Tuesday open mic in Gulfport. The pair are very confident singing on the microphone and have nice harmonies. Evidently, the guitar player has removed the low E string and the A string from his guitar. Bill tells me that this duo hosts an open mic at the beach on Sundays — another spot to visit sometime soon. They do a really interesting version of "Amazing Grace" and then another original, for a total of four songs.

The next performer is the guy that I said was kind of like James Taylor or Jackson Browne from the Brewers Tasting Room. He has an introspective style and plays original songs. Everyone has been doing four, but this guy does five because our host asks him to do one more.

Our featured performer has taken the stage to play a half-hour set, doing a mix of covers and originals and telling some stories. He calls out another local gigging musician who also hosts open mics, and then he calls me out as the guy who writes the books. When the host realizes who I am, he comes over to talk to me because he's a member of the SAM social media group. Overdue Bill and Steady Eddie are also members of that group. It doesn't blow my cover, though, because they don't know what I'm doing; they just recognize me from the books.

Overdue Bill plays till 9:10, and the next performer takes the stage with an Alvarez guitar to play original songs.

The guy who does the Pirates of Tampa song is using a Taylor guitar and has his harmonica around his neck. Before he goes up, I ask that he play that song because it was so fun last week.

We leave the open mic just before 10 PM. It is scheduled to last from seven to eleven, but we had our fill of food, drink, and music for the evening and it was time for us to head home. It was a quality experience overall. The venue was really cool, the host did a great job with the sound (it never got too loud), and there were good musicians sharing their music. I was very happy to find this open mic.

KAHUNA'S

It's been raining all day and I already know we're going to be walking and driving through a big storm. Rocky picks me up at 5:30 and we arrive at Kahuna's at 6:30. The open mic/jam starts at 7:00 and continues to 11:00. It is hosted by Charles, the host of the Brewers Tasting Room open mic last week. This is his new Thursday night location, after nine years at Brewers. This place is jamming — the parking lot is very full. We have to park on the grass.

This restaurant/bar is located on Gandy Boulevard, a road that turns into a bridge across the bay to Tampa. It's right around the corner from Brewers Tasting Room and McArthur's.

There are three high-top tables right next to the music area and a big horseshoe-shaped bar with an extension. We grab a couple of seats at the bar, off to stage right. There's also a covered front and back porch patio. On the other side of the bar area are several low tables, but we couldn't sit there because we wouldn't be able to see over the people sitting at the bar. All the way across the room are a few games including three pool tables.

Rocky signs up for the 7:45 slot on the list and tells me that they are doing 15-minute slots. Charles has one speaker up on a stand and another on the floor as a monitor. The last time we saw him he was using a pad to do the mixing, and he is using it again. There is also the same small drum set and the same drummer all set up and ready to jam.

Charles is playing an Allman Brothers song as a sound check. There is no stage, but there's actually a lot of room for the musicians to play and we're not sure if this venue has music regularly or not.

Rocky left his tuner on the table at the open mic last night so the waitress gave it to Steady Eddie, who reached out to Rocky on social media and let him know that he had it. He is supposed to come here tonight and play, so he will bring it with him. That's a great example of networking and community, and a little bit of good luck.

I meet Larry Lynch, who is a local musician and a member of my SAM social media group, but someone I've never met in person. He is wearing a Dancing SAM t-shirt from my merch store. That's the first time I've seen somebody out in public whom I don't know at all, wearing one of the SAM T-shirts. It's a really cool feeling. It would be like being in a band and walking through the mall and seeing a complete stranger wearing your T-shirt. He has his guitar and has signed up on the list.

A couple of other people with guitars have just shown up. I recognize one of them from Brewers Tasting Room. This is all part of being a part of the local musician community.

It's 7:00 and Charlie's still checking the sound, but it looks like he's getting ready to start playing some songs. Charles is very confident and loud on the microphone, making some announcements and letting the crowd know what is going on this evening.

A few other people with guitars have come in and signed up to play. A bass player has also arrived. It is a very loud crowd. The people talking are creating a high level of noise.

Our first act is a solo acoustic musician with a Taylor guitar and a mic stand attachment for his Pad, plus a couple of foot pedals. He plays three original songs, and the host adds lead guitar, making it a duo.

Our next act is a band: drums, bass, and two acoustic guitars. The jam includes both Charles and Steady Eddie. Two more musicians I recognize from Brewers have come in. The band gets started right away; Charles is playing lead, using a wah effect on his acoustic guitar.

From what I can tell, the band part of the show is a feature because they paused the list and just brought these guys up. The music is extremely loud and not exactly what I was looking for. I check the restaurant's website and see that it's advertised as a jam.

They play four songs and announce themselves as the BTR Project, which I believe stands for Brewers Tasting Room, where they probably jammed every Thursday night for years.

It is 10 after 8:00 and we are back to the list. I thought they would go right to Rocky but a guy with an acoustic guitar is tuning while music plays through the speakers. He's a solo act, and halfway through his first song the microphone cuts out. One of the patrons at the bar yells, "We can't hear his voice," but they get it fixed. He is playing some upbeat '90s alternative rock songs and the crowd is loving it. Like I said before, it's kind of a rowdy crowd tonight, but they are responding well, clapping and even singing along, so that's a really good thing, actually. He plays four songs.

There's more break music, then our host makes a couple of announcements and Rocky takes the stage. He plays three songs, and the next performer is a familiar face from Brewers Tasting Room: the guy who plays fingerstyle classical guitar. He does a little bit of a sound check and sets his small four-pedal board down on the ground. Our host introduces him almost like it's a boxing match or something. "People, are you ready for our next act, mister…" During one of his instrumental songs, he uses an effect that gives his guitar a lot of sustain. It is very cool when his low notes keep going as he picks out upper-register melodies on top.

There are quite a few TVs around the bar, the pool tables, and the other tables. But in the stage area, where they have the music going on, the TVs are turned off, and I think that's pretty cool. I also notice that they normally have tables in that space, but they moved them outside so the musicians could have a place to set up.

After Rocky's set, a few people come over to talk to him while he's trying to get his guitar packed up and out to the car. While he was playing and when he was outside talking with people and putting his guitar away, several people tried to take his chair to the other side of the bar or sit in it. I had to do the old "my friend will be right back" thing.

The finger-picking classical guitar guy is making beautiful music but the crowd doesn't seem to care much. I start clapping pretty loudly at the end of his song, and Rocky joins me, as do two other people at the bar. It's a really cool sound he's making, especially on his last two songs where there's a low, sustained drone from the low notes of the chords while he is picking out other notes. It sounds almost like a cello or a low violin so I'm sure it has something to do with his pedalboard. I'm not sure how to describe it but it's almost like a New Age style.

I hear the drums and bass warming up for the next performance and there is a solo acoustic guitar player in front of the microphone getting tuned up, so I think this is going to be a three-piece jam.

We leave at 9:00 because it's just too aggressively loud. We can't understand any of the lyrics and it's time to go. Maybe I have become an old fuddy-duddy, but I like the quieter open mics. I notice that a few people who were sitting up front at the high-top tables have moved to the other side of the room, by the pool tables.

My honest assessment of tonight is mixed. There were things I liked and things I didn't like. The host does a good job with the sound system, but it's too loud with the band/jams and that's not really what I'm looking for. I am purposely avoiding jam nights that are advertised as such. I will be going to some more open mics, and we'll see what we find there.

ALL 5 ELEMENTS

Rocky and Sue pick me up at 6:00 to go about 30 minutes south to All 5 Elements, a metaphysical shop in Largo. The sign outside says Crystals and Kava. They sell crystals, pendulums, and books, as well as Kratom and Kava. They do have some snacks, too. The website said the open mic starts at 7:00 but when we arrive, a chalkboard by the front door says 8:00 so I ask the woman behind the bar about the start time. She says 8:00, so we decide to go somewhere else and kill some time and come back.

We get back to the venue at 7:30 and there are a few more people there. The host is setting up some mic stands, a music stand, and a few other things.

Our host's name is Fred and at 10 minutes to 8, he points out where Rocky and Sue can sign up. He says that he will play a few songs to start the night and then start getting people onstage.

Including the lady behind the bar, there are 11 people in the room and our host is doing a little bit of a sound check.

A guy who had come in to sit at the bar with his laptop has just pulled a guitar that I couldn't see behind some clothes for sale off the wall next to the stage. He is sitting on one of the couches in front of the stage and playing along with the host.

There are some mural-type paintings on the wall, and what appear to be local artists' paintings for sale in the hallway by the bathrooms. The PA looks like a 4-channel Behringer powered mixer and there's one monitor on the floor that is aimed out towards the room that I believe is a Behringer as well. The small corner stage is about eight inches off the ground. I am at a high-top table behind some couches, and the venue has an eight-seat bar. Another part of the room is more of a shop, with all the things I listed earlier.

Our host plays six songs in about 25 minutes, then turns on some music while Rocky and Sue set up to play their songs. It's not too loud and you can hear the guitar and the vocals clearly, which is nice. It is not a very large room, so I'm happy that it's not too loud.

Rocky and Sue are playing the same three or four songs they did the other week at McArthur's. They sound good. The host wants them to do one more, but they played their four and that was the end of their set.

Another guy shows up with a guitar case and signs up on the list. I believe our bartender has also signed up to sing to music played from her phone.

As our next act begins his first song, another guy comes in without a guitar case — he knows the host and they bump fists. The SAM on stage plays five original songs on an Ibanez brand guitar. I hear our host tell him that he might be able to go back up again later if more musicians don't arrive.

We load out Rocky's guitar and Sue's harp, and now we're going to hang out for a little while and listen to the other musicians.

The next performer is our bartender. She is playing an instrumental track of a popular country song from her phone, which is plugged into the PA, and singing to it. She does a second song, by Hootie and the Blowfish. Our host Fred tells Rocky that they've been doing this open mic on Saturdays for about three and a half months so far. I was wondering how long they had been doing it, based on the turnout — it usually takes some time to get the word out about an open mic.

The next guy to take the stage is playing a Martin cutaway and he is left-handed. I think that's the first time we've encountered a left-handed player at any of these open mics. He asks if we don't mind if he plays an oldie. Sue recognizes the song, but we don't know who sang it. It's by the band America. He proceeds to play five or six songs, including a Beatles song.

We've had a couple of customers leave and we've had a couple of customers come in that aren't musicians. I go to the bathroom and when I come back there's a new guitar and two new guys hanging out on one of the couches. I don't know if they play music or not yet. One of the people who signed up decides not to play and one new guy gets on stage. His buddy goes outside and returns with a Gibson electric. I see two more customers come in, and a family of four with the dad carrying a guitar case.

For some reason, it gets really loud out of nowhere. I guess the host turned it up two or three times as loud as it was before. So we decide to leave, but it is actually picking up, with more people coming into the shop. When we walk outside there is a full moon and we joke about leaving the witch's shop on a full moon before it gets to midnight. We had planned on staying till 10:00 but leave about 9:45 — it's a small room and it just got really loud.

OZONA BREWING COMPANY

Rocky picks me up at 4:15 and we drive to the Ozona Brewing Company which is a brewery located in Palm Harbor, 1.3 miles from my house. In Ozona, which is the neighborhood next to mine, there are several restaurants on a main street surrounded by residential homes.

A local SAM that I know is playing on the front porch outdoor stage while the open mic is getting set up inside. This open mic is being hosted by Charles from the BTR and Kahuna's. That's how we found out about it. The SAM out front plays from 2 to 5, and the open mic is from 5:00 to 8:00.

When we walk into the main room and look for seats at a high-top table, Charles is hooking up speaker cables. There are two speakers attached to brackets bolted onto the ceiling. They look like QSC 10s with a horn. It is hard to tell. He's using two Alto speakers as monitors, and has a couple of mic stands and microphones. The back walls of the stage are covered in sound-proofing foam. He has been mixing from a pad the last two times we've seen him, and will be doing the same thing today.

I sit at a table with a woman who has brought her guitar, while Rocky gets his guitar from the car. Another woman with a guitar comes over and introduces herself, and the two ladies are talking about music. Evidently, the second lady and her husband are going to play from 5:00 to 5:30, so maybe that's a special feature performance.

The lady we are sharing the table with and Rocky sign up on the list. In the past, Charles has given out 15-minute slots, but we're not sure if that will be the format today because of the thirty-minute special performance.

Two other men with guitars have signed up to play. The musician on the front porch has finished his set and Charles is playing some music from his Pad through the stage speakers. Another guy with a guitar case is signing up on the list and the SAM out front is playing another song, so it seems like it'll be a relaxed transition from one event to the other.

A guy who has been helping Charles set up has a mandolin and a resonator-type dobro guitar. So that is something new. And our first act is going to be a husband-and-wife duo. She's playing acoustic guitar and he's the one with the mandolin and the dobro guitar. He puts his guitar across his hip so that he could play slide like a lap steel type situation; he's got fingerpicking picks on several fingertips and has a slide in his left hand.

It's a quarter after five and they've been doing a lot of soundchecking. The SAM out front played one more song after 5:00, and then packed up. There seems to be some dispute over whether or not one of the monitors is working or turned on or not.

Charlie introduces our first act and the music starts. The husband plays the first two songs on mandolin, and now they are doing an original where he is playing the acoustic slide dobro. He stays on the dobro for some more songs, including another original or two. They are doing a half-hour set. For their last song, the husband switched from dobro guitar to a diatonic blues harmonica.

A familiar face from both of the other open mics Charlie runs comes in through the back door with his guitar case.

Another woman has arrived with a guitar case and is signing up on the list.

Rocky has switched positions on the list with the woman we're sharing the table with — he will go first and she will follow him. So he's up after the husband-and-wife duo.

When Rocky gets on stage it's funny because of where Charles has placed one of the mic stands. Rocky is more than six feet tall. I think he used to be 6'6" and is now 6'3". We all shrink a little when we get older. The stage has four large Edison-style bulb-type lights spread out across the ceiling. The host set the mic stand up so one of the big light bulbs is right above Rocky's head, and it's very cartoonish, as if he has a bright idea. Rocky does three songs, after which our host comes to the stage to mute him and get him unplugged.

The crowd has been engaged and is clapping it up for each act so far, which is great. The outdoor front patio kind of died off after the other SAM packed up but there is a full tap room by the indoor stage.

There's some interim break music between acts and now they're tweaking the sound again. The nice lady who was sharing a table with us is playing a Dreadnought acoustic and it looks like our host Charlie is going to join her on his guitar. She's going to do four original songs.

A guy I know just got here but didn't bring his guitar in or sign up. He used to come to an open mic I hosted long ago, and play with a partner. He recognizes Rocky and starts talking to him. Rocky introduces us and he acts like he doesn't know who I am, and then he figures it out. "Oh wow!" he says, and I say, "Yeah, it's probably been eight or nine years since we've seen each other."

Our next act is playing a Takameni brand guitar and doing country songs. After the second song, he asks Charlie, over the microphone, "How many songs are we doing today?" Charlie replies, "Three." The guy drops his pick, so he stops playing for a second and everybody wonders what's happened as he bends down to pick it up. He starts right back into the song he was playing.

Rocky and I think the next SAM who took the stage is playing a Martin guitar, but there's a capo on the headstock which makes it hard to be sure. He plays very folky songs. Eventually he removes everything — he had a tuner and a capo on there, and now we can see that it is a Martin because he is using just the capo on the third song.

The next performer is another Solo Acoustic Musician, who has put a pad on the holder attached to the stand and is playing an Ibanez brand guitar. He gets to play a fourth song, as our host was chatting with one of the other musicians and wasn't really paying attention. That was fun because he played some '90s radio hits.

The next SAM on the stage is also playing what we think is a Martin. He is very confident on the microphone and starts his set with a country song followed by a rock song and then a blues tune.

The next performer is the guy we have seen play classical a couple of times with the four-pedal board; this time he's on an acoustic Seagull steel string guitar. He plays a beautiful finger-picking instrumental that is received very well. People are clapping between each of his songs. By his third instrumental he has really captured the audience's attention.

Charles announces that there are 12 people on the list tonight, and that when he started this event there were only four people the first time. This open mic is getting better and better every week.

The next act to take the stage is a duo — a female SAM and a male lead guitarist. Charles does a little bit of a sound check for them by adjusting the levels of the guitars and the microphones. They announce that they are going to play a few original songs that they have written together.

We cut out at 7:30. The open mic goes till 8:00, but I think I'm getting a little bit burnt out after going to so many. I think it's time to go get some dinner. I'll be back at it tomorrow night.

THE CHILL ROOM

FRIDAY, JUNE 9TH, 2023
PINELLAS PARK, FLORIDA

It's Friday night and Rocky picks me up at 6:30. We are going to the Chill Room in Pinellas Park which is a Kava house, smoke shop, and art studio where they blow glass and make things. There is supposed to be a cafe of some kind but to be honest, we are not sure what to expect.

The same guy that hosted at the metaphysical shop is the host here; we'll see what kind of PA system he has and what musicians show up to perform. We arrive at 7:11 and the event starts at 8:00, so we check in and hang out.

It's a pretty nice room with a real stage. The host has a couple of 15" Rockville brand speakers with horns on stands. There is a monitor on the stage and a music stand, and he is setting up two microphones. He has the same Rockville 4-channel powered mixer that he had last Saturday night, which is set up in the back of the stage area. There is a pool table between us and the stage which is interesting. It's right in front of the stage but off to the right.

It's a Kava & Kratom place (see the venue list and descriptions in SAM 2 where Chase Harvey describes these kinds of venues...) and they have lots of different drink choices, some baked goods, and some small snacks. They list pizza, chicken fingers with fries, and other appetizer-style items on the menu. To be honest, I have no idea what a lot of the drinks on the menu are, but it also includes coffee, lemonades, and more. Rocky orders an iced coffee and I drink some Gatorade.

We take a table by the door. There is a 14-seat bar along the back wall, and other tables and couches throughout the room. It's a very peaceful environment. While we're settling in, another musician I remember from the metaphysical shop shows up with a guitar.

At 7:40 our host tells Rocky that he's put the list at the end of the bar closest to the stage. About five minutes later, another man walks in with a guitar case and his girlfriend or wife. We move over to some really comfortable chairs that circle a small round table and now I have a direct view of the stage. One mic stand has a pad holder on it, and he has also put one of the nice high-top bar stools with a back on the stage if anybody wants to sit. Our host has a small tip can with blinking lights, and a clear acrylic 8 ½" x 11" sign with a code for people to tip him.

Rocky tells me he is second on the list. I point out a guy covering the pool table so nobody can play while the musicians are on. We thought that was very respectful of the musical acts.

It's 8:00 and our host has been soundchecking for a couple of minutes with his guitar; he starts singing promptly at 8:00. The lady from the Pesky Pelican open mic/jams with a djembe drum has just come in and is setting up on the stage. She immediately starts jamming along with our host.

Rocky leans over and tells me that he thinks it's cool that there are no TVs in the room. But he has his back to the bar area, and I point out three TVs up there, but they're all set on beach videos and things like that, not sports or TV shows.

This is a totally different environment than what we're used to seeing in restaurant or bar venues.

Another guy has been hanging out with the host and is invited up on stage. He has a little backpack full of harmonicas. Our host announces that if anybody wants the percussion woman to play with them, just ask her. After four songs together, they're done and the harmonica player is going to perform. He is using Bluetooth to play a track from his phone and he'll play harmonica along with it. He starts off with a Stevie Wonder song and he's using a chromatic harmonica.

A few people leave the venue, and a few others arrive. There are around twenty people in the room. It's not super busy but there is an audience. It's a pretty laid-back place — after all, it is called The Chill Room.

A guy who came in and signed up without a guitar went outside and just came back in with two. It seems to be a common theme at all the open mics we've been going to that people come in and sign up, sit down, and bring in their guitars later.

Our harmonica player did four songs and the djembe drummer played along with him. Now it is Rocky's turn. The host adjusts the mic stand for him; Rocky's sitting on the high-top bar stool. He does four songs, but then our host turns around from his conversation with another musician and says, "Do another one, please." So he is doing a fifth.

Our next act is one of the people from last Saturday and the djembe player is playing along with him as well. Once again, this event is not really what I was looking for. This guy is playing an original song, and I was hoping to hear it clearly, with just him playing. It is what it is, though; it's out of my control, so I'm just enjoying the music the way it is being presented.

Our host asks the guy to play one more song, giving him five, too. I don't know how many people are on the list, but I guess he's trying to make sure he fills the time.

Our next act is a male-female duo. He's playing an electric guitar, maybe a Guild semi-hollow body, that's kind of a blue-green color. He sets up a pedal board and they put a pad on a stand. The woman is going to sing while he plays guitar.

There is a little bit of a crowd buzz now — people are talking during and in between the songs, a little more than they were before, and one of the guys in the audience is tuning a 12-string guitar. That's the first of those that we've seen in our travels. There are about 30 people in the room at 9:20.

Our host does a little sound check with the singer's microphone and the electric guitar, trying to set a balanced mix. I see the woman has brought her own microphone. Once again, the djembe player is going to play along with another act. The guitarist is playing with a little bit of distortion, and it's kind of an alternative pop-rock style song. So, something a little different from the other acoustic folky people. For the third and fourth songs, the man takes over lead vocals and the woman adds harmonies on the choruses, and it sounds pretty nice.

Our next performer is a teenage girl with an acoustic-electric guitar. She sits on the chair while the host gets her microphone positioned and one of the other guys is helping her get tuned up. Maybe a little bit of mentoring is going on. Her father has pulled a low chair up to the front of the stage to shoot video of his daughter's set.

I'm trying not to write about negative things, but two things happen during her fourth song. Three other guys pulled out a guitar and start playing, and I can hear them as well as I can hear her. Another guy orders a pizza from a shop in the same strip mall, and gets it delivered to the venue. That's bad etiquette, because this place has pizza on its menu.

I'm not being judgmental, but it's something I wouldn't do myself, and I consider both these things bad etiquette.

The girl performs a fifth song and then a sixth, as the host is caught up in conversation with somebody else at the bar. Then she asks, "Should I stop?" Finally her parents say something to our host and he responds, "Oh, just do one more."

This could rebound badly for the host. It is possible that somebody else will get upset because they don't get to play, because time runs out, or maybe they won't get to play as many songs as the girl.

Two other guys roll into the venue with guitar cases and sign up on the list. I recognize one of them from a long time ago when I used to host open mics, but he doesn't recognize me. He spots Rocky and comes over to our table to say hi to him, though.

The teenage girl got the best sound of the night. I don't know if the host made changes to the PA or what, but her guitar and vocals sounded better than anybody else.

The djembe player takes the stage again, and the man that owns the 12-string sits on the bar stool and does a little soundcheck with our host. They move the second microphone to the other side of the stage for the teenage girl to sing along. This is a very experienced guitar player, and they definitely know each other. She sings one song with them and even splits lead vocal duties on the second verse.

It's 10:30 and there are still five or six people who haven't played. I don't know how they'll fit them in by 11:00, but we're heading out.

As we drive home, Rocky observes that quite a few times over many years of going to open mics, when somebody's doing really well, the crowd is clapping a lot for them, and they sound good, the host might just let them continue on for another extra song or two. That's clearly what happened tonight.

MICKY QUINN'S

Rocky comes by my house at 6:15 and we head to Micky Quinn's in Seminole, which is about a mile inland from the beach. We pull into the parking lot and as we're getting out of the car, another guy with a backpack guitar case heads inside, too.

When we walk into the bar we see some dart boards to the right and some high-top tables, along with a big fireplace and a U-shaped bar. We don't see any music equipment so we walk around the other side of the bar. There we find the open mic and the other musicians who are already there. It's nice and dark, but they've got some stage lights on. There's a fan on the ceiling of the stage and a couple of speakers attached to the walls. They look like QSC 12s with horns and there's a monitor on the stage. Our host has a mixer on a bar stool in front of him to run sound from in front of stage right.

It's a really cool environment — they even have some kind of theatrical stage dressing on the sides and up across the top, which is a neat feature. I grab a high top as far away from the stage as possible; there are big wooden tables and stools.

All the flyers I saw said that the event was scheduled for 7:30 to 11:00, but our host is singing a Johnny Cash song for the sound check. They continue to sound check as a duo. Our hosts tonight are Paper and Strings, the duo I saw the other night. Their real names are Adam and Christy.

Adam is making some announcements, letting everybody know it's an open mic and they can sign up to perform. Then he invites Christy up to the stage.

There are about 10 other people around the bar, having after-work beers and relaxing in the air conditioning. It's another hot day here in Tampa Bay.

Our hosts announce that they're going to play one more song, which will be their third, and then bring up the first performer on the list.

The first performer is a Solo Acoustic Musician playing a 12-string guitar and using a vocal harmonizer. I'm not sure at first if he's using a pedal, or if the host turned it on for him with the mixer.

After his first song, I see him step on the ground behind the monitor, and the vocal harmonizer effect is gone. So it was a pedal that I didn't notice him bring to the stage. He turns it back on during his second song. Both of those were '70s rock songs. His third song is in the same genre — he is singing the verses without the harmonizer, only turning it on during the choruses. He plays five songs and then they make some announcements about his social media.

The host team is pretty good. Christie adjusts the microphone stand and gets the next performer ready and checks the list, while Adam is making announcements about each night of the week here at Micky Quinn's. The next performer's last name is O'Reilly and he's from Ireland. I think he's playing a Martin acoustic-electric, and he is a SAM.

He is strumming along to authentic Irish songs, using a pick that wraps around his thumb. He's also using a capo for each song, moving it up and down the neck.

I head to the bar to order us some seasoned fries and Guinness dipping gravy, and the night's first performer comes to our table and is talking with Rocky about music. It is amazing how many people Rocky seems to know from years of going to open mics — almost everywhere we've been, he's known one or two people.

After Mr. O'Reilly's fifth song, the host helps him make announcements about a few upcoming gigs at some other Irish bars in Pinellas County or in the St. Petersburg area just south of here. The host asks him to do one more, then makes a nice request for everybody to clap. He puts on some break music and another Solo Acoustic Musician steps up.

This is our second open mic at an Irish bar, and each has provided an actual stage dedicated to music. Each has provided some or all of the PA speakers. Each has had liquor, beer, wine, and a kitchen with a pretty nice authentic Irish-themed menu. If I were hoping to host an open mic, these places are checking off almost all the boxes.

The guy onstage is doing cover songs, but he throws in one original about his favorite car. After four songs he says, "I'm done." Our host once again gets everybody to make some noise and tells the performer to announce his upcoming gigs or social media.

Christie runs a cable to a second mic stand because we're going to have a duo: a man playing guitar and a woman who is going to accompany him on vocals. Once again, there's break music being played while they switch out and both people are adding iPad holders and iPads to the mic stands. The guitar player does a little soundcheck, stepping on a pedal that makes a bass drum sound. He has it plugged into the PA. We haven't seen that before in our open-mic adventures.

Christie comes over to tell Rocky that he is up after this act, and he can have up to 20 minutes. If he wants to, he can play less, just let her know. Adam introduces the duo act.

The woman is singing lead and the man is playing acoustic guitar with his bass drum stomp box pedal thing and he sings harmony on the chorus of their first song.

Between their third and fourth songs, they grab everyone's attention by saying that if you type their name into any search engine, they will come up first. Obviously, they have put in the effort to get to be #1, but I admit it is a really cool marketing ploy and I would bet that they do it at every open mic and every gig they play. It's a unique and smart move!

Their first song was from *The Godfather*. They are very entertaining because they are dancing and interacting with the audience after each song. They are a well-rehearsed, polished act.

Rocky is next, and he's going to play four or five songs with his classical guitar.

At this point, I think there's only one person on the list after him, but I'm not sure. It's a pretty cool place and I'm surprised that it's now 8:43, and that there aren't more people here because we are surrounded by residential neighborhoods. I have to remind myself that it is Tuesday, which is one of the slower nights of the week.

Rocky plays four originals and one cover. His first original is a song he wrote for Paper and Strings — of course, they really like it, and so do all the other people. Everyone thought it was cool and he gets a lot of applause.

The next performer is playing a Takamine brand guitar. I think he's the last person on the list tonight, and it's 9:00. Our host duo is going to play some more songs for the people in the audience.

In the space of five minutes about twenty new people fill in the other side of the bar and the high-top tables in the dining room.

At 9:15, I pay the check, and we're out.

THE HAUS COFFEE SHOP & WINE BAR

Today we're going to a place in Indian Rocks Beach, just south of Clearwater Beach, called The Haus Coffee Shop and Wine Bar. The open mic starts at 7:00 and goes to 10:00. Rocky grabs me up at 5:30 — we're going to make a stop in Clearwater Beach, where I have a five-minute meet-and-greet with a bar owner at 6:00.

The previous bar in that location closed and he opened up an Irish-themed bar/restaurant in the same spot. After that, we will head down Gulf Boulevard along the beaches and cross the bridge at Walsingham Road back to the mainland, just across the bridge, where the coffee shop is located.

The owner I was supposed to meet is not at the bar in Clearwater Beach, so I leave a card with one of the bartenders and email him to let him know that I came by. We head to Indian Rocks Beach and arrive at the coffee house at 6:17.

When we walk in, we pass under an archway and see a mixer mounted on the wall for the host to use. The stage area is clearly designated for live music. It has two main speakers on stands attached to the wall, and there are two monitor speakers on the stage.

Our host tonight is named J., and he is setting up two microphone stands, checking them by going back and forth to the mixer. There are already four or five guitar cases here in the room and some friends and family are with the performers. I see Melanie, the woman that plays the djembe drum, is here and has her djembe set up on the stage already. She clearly goes to a lot of open mics because this is the third or fourth place we've seen her, and she was at the Pesky Pelican every time we went there.

I order an apple juice and get Rocky an iced tea. I am directed to the chalkboard menus in the other room where coffee and food can be ordered. They have a breakfast menu that's not available right now, and a range of sandwiches for lunch and dinner, plus lots of wine and beer options. It's a pretty cool environment. There's a lot of wood on the wall and the color scheme gives it a very comfortable vibe and feel.

I spot a flyer for a Junior Open Mic event on Tuesday nights. It is for younger musicians — seventeen and under — and it runs a little earlier in the evening, from 6:30 to 9. It says PA, stage, and piano provided. They do have a piano against the wall at the back of the stage. That's something unique I've never seen before.

At 6:30 our host brings out a white marker board and puts it on the table right next to the front-of-house mixer. He waves it around for everybody to see and people jump up to sign onto the list.

Rocky's been off to the side of the stage, where there is something like a green room. It has some couches and end tables where people can relax. Our host is playing a song while one of the other friends and performers is helping with the soundcheck. Rocky tells me that the duo from last night is here, a man playing guitar and a female singer that were very entertaining.

About five minutes to 7:00, the host comes over and says, "Hi Mike. Are you going to play tonight?"

I reply, "No. I didn't bring my guitar."

He says, "Well, you can use my old Gibson. I'd really love to have you play."

I tell him I didn't think he recognized me because I haven't seen him in so many years and he says, "Well, if you change your mind, I could use a couple more players tonight."

I ask how many people are on the list and he says six so far. I tell him to give everybody an extra song to help fill the time. Then we talk about Gibson guitars for a few minutes, and I tell him I've found one that I want: the Songwriter. He heads back to the stage to start right at 7:00.

There are a few people here who were at the Irish bar, Micky Quinn's, the night before. That makes sense because the two venues are not very far apart geographically.

Our host starts playing a song that features harmonica. Before he starts, he announces that they are giving each performer three songs tonight, adding that we'll see how it goes and people may have an opportunity to play a second time if they get through the list quickly.

During his first song, Mark Hanson shows up to say hi, and two other guys arrive, sign up, and greet a couple of other musicians. It definitely seems like all the musicians know each other and there's a feeling of community at all these open mics. Everybody that gets here says hi to somebody else and then finds a place to sit.

The host plays his three songs. One is in a finger-picking style and the others are flat-picking. They're folky, story-style singer-songwriter songs and afterward he announces who is up next.

He puts a sock-like thing on the microphone, and I wonder if he's going to do this for everybody or just one time. Now he's at the mixer on the wall, helping our next act with a sound check. The guy who has the female singer as a partner has set up a video camera to the right of the stage on a small tripod — they did that last night at the Irish bar, but I think he just videotaped their own performance.

Our host introduces a Solo Acoustic Musician who says he's going to sing some folk songs and tell some stories. He tells a story about hanging out with John Prine one night in Chicago and sharing each other's songs all throughout the evening, and then plays a John Prine song.

There's only one TV here and it is showing the various menus of products that are available, from food to coffee to other drinks. It is nice to be in a venue that does not have a lot of TV screens playing sports or shows. The focal point is the music.

Mark Hanson stays for a little bit and says hi to almost every musician in the room because he knows everybody. He tells me that he's tired from a long day so he's heading home. It's 7:24 and our second act is in the middle of their second song. They play three cover songs, then our host calls Rocky up to the stage and announces the name of the act on deck. Rocky sits on a low chair and the host lowers the mic stand for him. Melanie the djembe player joins him for his set.

Our host uses a microphone from the front-of-house mixer to announce the next person and say, "Everybody put your hands together and make a round of applause for so-and-so." He also announces the next act as well as the person on deck which is something we haven't seen before. It's a good way of letting the musicians know to get their guitars tuned and be ready.

The performer after Rocky has been playing a twelve-string guitar for years and lets everybody know he's playing a six-string tonight. After that Melanie the djembe player and the man who plays guitar and sings with the female vocalist. He is sitting in on lead guitar with another woman who plays guitar and sings. The woman's guitar is not putting out any sound, and the man gives her his guitar and borrows another from the host. After a little bit of sound check, we can now hear everyone and they're rocking in an old-timey acoustic blues/jazz-type jam.

Another guy who is just a fan or customer tells the host that he should mic the djembe. I don't think that is necessary in this room. Suddenly, there's a bunch of feedback. The mic position is wrong and he's turned it up too much. He turns it back down and the feedback goes away.

Rocky orders a BLT and chips and sits at a low table up front to eat. I'm sitting at the wine bar in the back, all the way across the room, because it is a little bit too loud for me up close. He comes to my table and tells me that the woman per-forming is a published jazz songwriter. The guitar player with her only did rhythm at the Irish bar, but he is actually quite an accomplished player, laying some bluesy and jazzy lead lines over her songs. The woman sings very well. It is quite a nice mix of musical styles tonight. They do a fourth song.

Melanie stays on stage to play with a man on acoustic gui-tar, and another man on a thin hollow-body electric guitar. There is a woman singing at center stage microphone. J does a little sound check for each instrument and microphone and the quartet proceeds to play some very jazzy standards.

After the four-piece finish their jazzy songs, we have the duo from last night with the female singer and the acoustic guitar player and singer, and Melanie is joining them on the drum. Their first song is about chocolate, which is something I've never heard before. After they play it, the female singer announces that it was written by the published jazz singer in the audience, and that she gave it to them a few months ago. They do their routine about internet searches for their name again, promising that if they don't come up number one, they'll buy you a drink. They are going to England for three months so our host announces, "Since they are going to be gone for a few months, let's hear them play another song." Everyone claps and they do a fourth song.

We have had a few customers and even some performers come and go, but there are twenty-six to thirty people here in the room. It's not a very big place so it's a nice turnout, and everybody has a drink or some kind of coffee drink and a sandwich or some kind of food. A woman I've never seen before brings a guitar in from a car outside and four or five non-music customers come in and order glasses of wine. Everyone is enjoying the music and paying attention to the performers.

The next performer is a SAM but he has Melanie playing along with him on her drum. Evidently, Rocky talked to him at some point tonight and he tells me that the guy plays lots of gigs on the beach areas near here. I'd never heard of him and was curious what he would sound like, and when he plays an old Robert Johnson song it's really good. I don't have a great view of the stage and couldn't tell immediately, but he set a loop and is playing slide guitar. I don't think we've encountered anybody playing slide lead guitar before tonight. It's an acoustic, but I believe it's a classical guitar because it definitely has nylon strings. He plays with a pick, not fingerpicking.

In between the second and third songs, he announces that he will be playing here Saturday night. He likes to play funky blues and one of his songs is about drinking beer.

By 9:15 they have gone through everybody on the list, so the host asks some of the people if they want to play another short set. Rocky and I decide to head home. I think that was probably the closest we've come to a Listening Room, as far as the layout, the PA system, and the stage, which wasn't raised up but was definitely a dedicated stage area with an archway over it. There's even some separation — a wall with archways and window-like areas for people to look through from back by the wine bar. Everybody in the main room was very quiet and attentive to the performers, though a few people in the back room talked during performances. It was laid out very nicely and very comfortably. I really enjoyed that particular open mic.

SNOOTY'S SOCIAL HOUSE

Rocky comes by my house at 6:10. We don't have far to go — the open mic is right in our neighborhood, at Snooty's Social House. They have high-end craft beer and wine, and are located in a strip mall that includes an Italian restaurant, a seafood restaurant, and some other businesses. We arrive at 6:30 and the event is supposed to be from 7:00 to 10:00.

It is a long skinny room, and the hosts are setting up at the far end. One of the guys is wearing a Jason Isbell T-shirt, which is kind of cool.

There are three guys in front of the stage area, talking about their guitars. I head to the left, to the end of the bar just inside the door so I can get a seat as far away from the music as possible. I can see there's some kind of speaker stick or line array PA. I just hope it's not too loud.

I am sitting behind a Frosty Drink Machine thing with two sides, one green, one red. I'm not sure what it makes — maybe some kind of margarita or something. I really want to order a bottle of water and have leaned over a few times, but the bartender hasn't really caught my drift or spotted me.

This place is two or three miles from my house, and was some kind of beer bar for a few years, but they closed. It became Snooty's several months ago. Right now, there are six regular customers and there are already six musicians.

Rocky and I both order non-alcoholic Heineken beer along with some tacos. I start talking to a couple of ladies at the bar who are here for the Snooty's wine deals. Since it seems that he knows two out of the three guys hanging out by the stage area, gear, and equipment, Rocky goes over to talk to them.

One of the hosts plays a song and it's not too loud, which makes me happy. I am able to have a conversation with the two women next to me, which is nice, and the tacos are really good. Our host asks if it's too loud or not loud enough, and I am more than happy to reply, "Thank you for not being too loud."

It's 7:05 and Rocky is sitting at a table in front of the stage with the other musicians, and I know he's first on the list. I see a few more musicians coming in the door with guitars and amps. I recognize one of them but it doesn't seem that he recognizes me. Another man with a guitar walks in with a woman — his girlfriend or duo partner.

Rocky plays his four songs and the line array PA system isn't too loud. I'm able to continue chatting with a woman named Lisa while her friend is outside on the phone. I start to feel like I'm blending in with the regular customer crowd. Remember that I am undercover, and am trying not to be singled out.

It seems like the musicians have congregated at the table in front of the stage, even though it's a long skinny room with plenty of other open seats and tables. Two more people with guitar cases come in, and I assume they are going to sign up on the list and play.

We're on the third act by just after 7:30, and Rocky is talking to one of the people who has just signed up on the list. Afterward, he comes over and we talk about the music.

I feel I am not that productive tonight. To be honest, I've been more engaged with the two women at the bar than the music. I am enjoying my conversation with them and I'm really enjoying just hanging out and being part of the crowd.

Our next performer's name is Picking Rick. So far, it's been nothing but Solo Acoustic Musicians, which is what I was hoping to see at these open mic night events. There are fifteen people in the room and it's a quiet night.

Our first duo of the night takes the stage next. The guy who's playing rhythm and singing used to come to my open mic night and I'm blessed, I guess, that he hasn't noticed or recognized me. His friend is playing lead lines on a hollow-body electric guitar.

A guy named Ray comes over to talk to me and Rocky during their songs. It is a little louder now, because the electric guitar player is using a separate amp rather than plugging into the host's PA. It seems that the volume is causing an issue with the restaurant next door.

The duo is on their fifth song I think and they're doing "Gloria" — you know, "G-L-O-R-I-A, Gloria."

I'm impressed by how clean and new this place seems. It was probably eight months ago when it changed hands or closed. It's just not a big turnout for a Tuesday, and I have to consider that maybe the open mic is still growing. I am sure some Tuesdays are busier than others. There are eighteen of us in the room and a few people have come and gone throughout the evening. It's still not too loud, and I appreciate that.

There are actually a few reasons why I don't sing at these open mic events. The first is that I don't bring my guitar, but another is that I don't bring my microphone, which is in my guitar case, or my iPad, which contains my songbook. I can do anything I want to do. In some of the places, the host will tell me that I can use their guitar and I always say no thanks. It's probably not tuned the way I like, down half a step. I could bring my lyrics up on my phone, which I did at the coffee shop in Indian Rocks, thinking I might actually go up and do a set. I looked up the three songs I wanted and found them on my phone. But I don't want my mouth anywhere near those microphones.

At 8:30, the solo acoustic performer onstage announces that he is playing here again later in the week. The sound was quite different during his set, and quite good — I could hear everything all of a sudden. Sometimes it's not the sound system and it's not the equipment or the person running it that is doing something wrong. It is the performer who is actively listening and adapting to the sound system.

A guy named Gary comes over and we chat about a bunch of stuff. He is the one who I recognized earlier, because he used to come to play at my open mic. Rocky tells me that he's going to play another set, and we're listening to another duo. They're not formal, but they sound pretty good and we're hearing some good music. Gary and I haven't spoken for a long time so we're catching up about different venues and places to play in the neighborhood.

I have enjoyed this open mic and I would definitely return to it again. I would even bring my guitar and microphone so I could play a few songs next time.

CROOKED THUMB BREWERY

TUESDAY, JUNE 27TH, 2023
SAFETY HARBOR, FLORIDA

I left my house at 6:00 and am driving to the other side of the peninsula where I live, to a little town called Safety Harbor. I've heard it got its name because the pirates would come up into Tampa Bay and park their boats there when the big storms came so they would be protected. I don't know if that's true; it could just be a fun tale that people tell. There are a lot of tales and folklore in the pirate world.

I'm headed to a place called The Crooked Thumb Brewery and I'm sure there's a story behind that name as well. At one of the Tuesday open mics, at the North End Tap House in St. Pete, the owner of this brewery showed up. I texted him that I was coming over, but he is on his way to Indiana and won't be in attendance. I will be talking to our host tonight. His name is Josh, and this is not an open mic per se but some kind of a singer-songwriter original showcase.

I arrive at 6:27 and our host is doing a sound check on the outside stage. He has been doing this event for quite a few years now — I was a featured performer once back in 2018 or 19, but we were inside. Since then, the brewery has added a good-sized outdoor stage with a covered roof. He has one speaker on a stand and another as a monitor, and two microphones set up.

When I did this event with him, there were three of us and we took turns doing our songs in the round, as they say.

He's using a pad of some kind to run his mixer. I approach the stage to say hi, and he shows me that he's using a wireless Behringer X-air PA head.

I was surprised that what I think is the format has changed, but in reality, I didn't remember the format. It used to be a featured performer in the round every other week, and was otherwise open for anybody to sign up on the list.

Rocky was going to meet me here without his guitar, but I call him and tell him to bring it if he wants to play. I guess they haven't been doing the showcase thing for a little while. I think I would have actually brought my guitar had I known, and I tell our host that, so he offers to let me play his.

I go inside to get a bottle of water and a general manager from a place I used to play is behind the bar. We don't recognize each other at first because it's been years since we have seen each other in person, but it's a nice added bonus to this adventure.

While I'm talking with our host, a woman with a guitar case comes in; I recognize her from years ago, but I know she doesn't recognize me. While I'm getting my water, another local gigging SAM comes in to get a beer and says he had planned on coming here to play but something is wrong with his guitar's electronics and he's taken it to the shop. I think our host will probably let him play his guitar as well, we'll see what happens.

It's been a hot day and it's beautiful out here, but it is warm. Our bartender told me he was going to let Josh set up inside, but he was already prepping the stage by the time he realized he was even here.

I move a table and chairs over next to the building, which is actually dead center straight out from the stage, but also only five feet from an electric outlet. Then I get both of my gig fans from my van, to put on me and whoever sits at my table. It will keep us cool and keep the bugs away.

Our host does some sound-checking with his guitar, trying a couple of cool effects. And promptly at 7:00 PM, he goes inside to cut off the house music and get started playing some songs.

Josh tells us that he's going to play some original songs and that the name of the event is the Melody Artisans of the Crooked Thumb, which is the fancy name for the songwriter's showcase.

During his first song, another fellow with a guitar case walks into the beer garden. I look around and see three different signs that say "Welcome to our beer garden" with a list of rules which is cool by me. They include keeping your dog on a leash, respecting the musicians on the stage, and a few other common-sense rules. I see a few customers have come from the air conditioning inside and out to the paved patio and are taking up a table with their beers to listen to the music, which is nice. I like when there are respectful customers who listen and clap at an open mic.

Another guy with a guitar case arrives and it seems like everybody knows each other. They all wave, shake hands, or hug and say hi. It's nice to see that sense of community.

During the host's second song, yet another person with a guitar case has shown up and signed up. The list is on the far corner of the stage, and it seems like every musician tonight knows right where to go. I think that puts us at eight musicians so far, plus our host. Almost all of them have brought a friend or family or some other people with them, which is great for the attendance numbers.

It sounds really good. Our host is doing a good job with the sound. I think this is very much the songwriter open mic format that I've been looking for during all these open mics I have been attending.

After our host's third song, he says, "I guess I'll do one more and everybody can do four songs tonight. It looks like it will be just enough of us on the list to fill out the time." Everybody claps for him and then he announces who the next performer will be.

When the next act plugs in and our host uses his Pad mixer to turn up the volume on the guitar, there's some kind of humming feedback, so Josh is switching out the cable and trying a different one. Now the guitar is coming in crystal clear, so something was going on with the connection. This performer has been directed to sing into the second microphone. Josh gives him an introduction, everybody claps, and he starts playing an original song in a folky singer-songwriter style.

A plane flies overhead, something I didn't make a note of the first two times it happened. This is to be expected, because we're near a couple of airports. Tampa International and Clearwater/St. Pete are not far from Safety Harbor. It isn't so loud that it drowns out the music, but it's something I haven't encountered in my adventures so far. During this performer's third song, Rocky shows up and pulls up a chair at my table. It's really nice that everybody's paying attention. As I look around the beer garden, there are at least twenty-five people outside, and everybody's really into the music. He's a very creative lyricist. Our host asks everybody to put their hands together for him as the next person prepares to play.

The next performer is using a Paul Reed Smith acoustic-electric and has a very unique voice. He is also playing original songs. During his first song, our host walks past my table with an XLR cable and throws it in the trash, saying that it was on the stage when he arrived tonight. He tested it out and it didn't work so into the trash it goes.

I step inside the taproom to get another bottle of water and they have opened up the big garage door so the people inside can hear the music as well. There are about 20 people inside, so this is a pretty good turnout for a Tuesday evening.

After his fourth song, the artist onstage passes his guitar to the woman with him. I recognize her from many years ago as a snowbird (somebody that comes to Florida during the winter times) but I think she lives here full-time now, and he is her son. She is also playing original songs and has started off with a finger-picking storytelling ballad. She plays four beautiful, very well-written originals in all.

I am very impressed with the level of songwriting here at this event. The creative lyrics, vocals, and guitar playing, added to well-crafted all-around song structures from each person so far, are a delight.

Rocky goes over to talk to her and her son while our host is preparing things for the next performer, the local working musician who didn't bring his guitar because it was in the shop. He's going to play Josh's acoustic. He sets up his fourth song by telling us that Josh used to put out prompts once a month or every other week, to give people a subject to write songs about, and this is a song he wrote when the subject was tattoos. They were doing this exercise for quite a while and it would help get people out of writer's block and give them some kind of mission-oriented songwriting task, which is a really creative idea and something totally different from all the other open mics I've been going to during this adventure that I'm on. Our host comes over to my table and we talk a little bit, and Rocky comes back and says, "Man, this guy sings really good."

Several more people have come out onto the patio by this time. It's after 8:30 and the sun has gone down behind the building. It has cooled off dramatically in the last half hour and there are some more customers that have brought their dogs and beers to the outside patio. Once again, we have a Solo Acoustic Musician playing original songs for our next act. I don't think anybody has played a cover song tonight so far.

The last guy's guitar was out of tune the whole time, but our next solo performer sounds decent. He is also doing original songs and plugs the band that he's in. His wife is at the front picnic table, using her phone to film his set.

Our host comes over at 9:00 and asks if either of us wants to play a song, so Rocky goes to his car and brings back a guitar that he just got. It is a Guild classical acoustic-electric guitar. I guess we're at the end of the list, but we still have a little bit of time left because the event usually goes to 9:30 or later if needed. But everybody's done four songs.

Rocky tunes up at the table. We are all the way across the beer garden from the stage, so he isn't bothering anyone. The moon is shining through a group of giant oak trees with Spanish moss hanging from them.

Rocky is on his fourth song, and I don't know if our host is going to play after him. There are still a couple of musicians hanging out. Nobody left right after they were done, so that's nice that they got the etiquette part right, and even the people that aren't musicians have been very polite, watching and clapping and listening without talking over everybody.

It's time for me to unplug my fan, put it in the van, and pay for my two bottles of water. The bartender comes out to gather up some empty glasses and says, "Dude, that's a pro move, you've got your own fan plugged into the wall."

I tell him, "I moved this table over close to the outlet so I could power it up."

He asks, "Do you keep that in the van all the time?"

I say, "I always have two of them in my van for gigs. I have even brought them out at restaurants here in Florida when I'm sitting in a tiki bar sometimes and it's just dead air hot. I'll plug them in where people plug in their cell phones."

Our host is strapping on a guitar and he's going to play for 15 minutes to fill the time till 9:30. I have to say that this has been one of my favorite events, just because it was all original music. The sound was good. There was a dedicated stage. It was really cool with all the lights around and it's cooled off temperature-wise too. It was a nice experience, and I would definitely bring my guitar to this event.

In between our host playing his first and second song, I go up and tell him I'm leaving and that everything sounded great. It was nice to see him again because it had been a while. I go inside to pay for my water and the bartender says, "What? Get out of here, you don't owe for a couple of bottles of water." That was nice. I really enjoyed the music tonight.

NOLAN'S PUB

Rocky and his wife pick me up around 6:45 and we drive to an Irish Pub named Nolan's in Safety Harbor. We arrive a little after seven, and there's an EV line array system set up along with two mic stands and a music stand up front, just inside the door to the left. I find a table for us in the back. Rocky's by the stage getting Sue's harp unpacked and set up. The host is helping them out and talking to them and another musician who's just arrived with his guitar case.

There are at least 28 people in here and it's a very small bar area, so it's quite crowded. All the bar seats and high tops are full but I find a table which is a low top in the back. I can't really see the stage area at all.

The host is named Jack — he was also the host at the Snooty's open mic last week. At 7:15 he starts playing, with someone on electric drums or some kind of drum machine.

I go to the bar to get a beer and see that it's a drum pad of some kind. They are playing a Beatles cover for their third song. The musicians aren't too loud, but the sound is very muffled and not too clean, so it's hard to understand the lyrics.

After their seventh song, the host announces that the performers who've signed up will start playing. Another guy has showed up with a guitar case on his back. I'm hoping that some people at one of the tables will leave so I can switch to a high top; I would like to be closer to the stage and be able to see things better.

The second act is a duo — a man playing acoustic guitar and a woman singing and playing the tambourine. During their third song, they do some decent harmonies in the choruses, which are nice to hear. Their fourth song is a cover of "Stormy Monday." During this song, the host comes back to our table to tell Rocky and Sue that there are a few more songs and then they can go up. He also introduces himself to another guy who came to the back area with his guitar; that guy's wife tells us that he hosts an open mic back home. They are visiting for the week from Rochester, New York. They have looked up open mics and are going around town to play various events as part of their vacation.

The duo finishes their set and says "Thank you, everybody, we're so and so, husband and wife duo team," and our host says, "Everybody make some noise for them," and we all clap.

The stage area is in a front window, looking right out onto the main street of Safety Harbor. It is a street that has a world-famous spa at the east end. All up and down it and on all the side streets are bars, restaurants, and stores of all kinds. The town is on the bay side of the peninsula and we are on the next-to-last block which ends at the spa, right on the bay.

I feel like a zoo animal stretching my head up over the fence trying to see from this short chair. I am trying to look past the people at the bar and the high-top tables so I can see what's going on. Somebody else comes in through the door and looks at the list and I think he signs up. He makes his way to the back area and realizes there's nowhere to sit, and that's when I see his guitar case.

Our third act is a Solo Acoustic Musician. I can't see what brand of guitar he's playing, but the crowd noise has picked up a little more because people are having their after-work beers in the pub. Every place we go and every situation is different. It's just something we have to adjust to. Our host comes back and tells Rocky and Sue they are up after this guy's fourth song, and asks them if they can do four songs tonight.

The husband-and-wife duo leave their high-top table, so I scoot up there to get a better view. Jack is running sound from right in front of the stage area, at the end of the bar. He starts a sound check for Rocky and Sue. There are some feedback problems, so he moves Rocky a little bit to the side, because the microphone is right in front of the line array system. It works and there is no more microphone feedback.

They receive a really nice welcome from the crowd and everybody claps. Jack points out that the bartender makes a joke — that this is the first time there's been a harp in Nolans that wasn't a beer, because they have Harp on tap. This might be the best that I've heard Sue's harp coming through from out in the crowd. She has joined us a few times now and this time it sounds particularly nice. The harp is featured, and the guitar is a little softer, but you can also hear Rocky's singing. It's quite well balanced and I am glad to be able to hear everything better from this new table.

I've never seen Jack go up on the stage to make any changes, I just see him hanging out in one spot, except to tell the next person on the list that they are next. He's using Wi-Fi to control the EV stick PA from a pad.

During Rocky and Sue's set, I go to the bar and get myself a Grandpa Jack's Pilsner, which is made by the Crooked Thumb Brewery where we were a couple of nights ago. I didn't have any beers that night, because I was driving, but Rocky and Sue picked me up for this event, so I thought I would enjoy a couple of beers and listen to the music.

Sue moves her harp off the stage and out of the way while Jack gets our next performer set up. He's a Solo Acoustic Musician, but the drum pad machine guy is going to join him. The intermission is a little bit longer because the harp, although small for a harp, is still a large instrument. Rocky likes to get it off the stage and into its case and take it to the car. He'll be back in a few minutes, as we are parked right across the street.

The host makes a big to-do about the next guy, and the music has picked up, both in volume and tempo. They're kind of rocking out. Of course, I did move up from the back of the room, so it's a little louder than before, but it sounds good. They play a really cool version of "Truckin'" by the Grateful Dead, but of the four songs he plays, two are originals.

The man from out of town is up next. He and his wife are sitting at the high-top table right behind me. When he gets up to make his way to the stage, as the other act is packing up, I notice the back of his guitar's headstock and ask him if it's a Takamine. He says yes, and that it's been hanging on his wall. "I've never actually plugged it in. I played it around the house on the couch." So he's interested to hear what it sounds like.

Of all the guitars tonight, this one sounds the best and I don't know if it's just the guitar and the settings on his active electronics. It must be, because I don't think our host made any major changes. His second song was one of the best of the night; he played Amos Lee's "Windows Are Rolled Down." I really love that song.

He's very good and the crowd is receiving him quite well, so I hope this is a highlight of his vacation from upstate New York to Florida. Jack asks him if he will play another song and the crowd cheers, so they really are enjoying what he's doing.

Our next performer is playing what looks like a Telecaster and the pad drummer is going to join him and make a duo out of it.

It's 9:30 and half the people have left. Our visiting guitar player came by almost every table to say goodbye to people; he and his wife said their kids are calling them. They're on vacation visiting family and it's 9:30 on a weeknight.

It was happy hour/dinnertime when everybody got here and was drinking beers and hanging out, and now it's the time of night when things are winding down. I know there's at least one more person on the list, but I'm not sure we're going to stay.

I pay for my beers and Sue's wine after they play, and we are headed home. They didn't have any food at Nolan's, but they did have a free popcorn machine. It is just a little neighborhood pub with beer and wine.

CHICAGO JAQX PIZZERIA AND TAPHOUSE

SUNDAY, JULY 9TH, 2023
INDIAN ROCKS BEACH, FLORIDA

Today we are going to an open mic at Chicago Jaqx Pizzeria and Taphouse. It runs from 3:00 to 6:00 PM. I guess this is an example of why you would not call it open mic *night* 'cause it's an open mic afternoon. (Imagine me saying that in the voice of the late great Mitch Hedberg.)

Rocky grabs me up at 2:15 and we drive through the mansions of South Bel Air Beach into Indian Rocks Beach. On the way, I think this event is hosted by Paper and Strings but when we get there it's Fred, whom we've met before at a couple of the other spots. I guess they have some kind of revolving host system.

When Rocky picked me up, I grabbed a couple of fans from my van and when we grab a table under the roof, in the shade of the deck patio area, I plug them in right away. Even though they have fans mounted in the roof it's nice for us to have our own. It is mid-July in Florida, and we are at the beach. It is over 90° today.

The stage area used to be a parking lot spot, which they have raised up and covered in fake grass and put a couple of umbrellas over it. Fred is once again using the Rockville 4-channel powered mixer with a Kustom monitor and two small 8" Harbinger speakers on stands. He already has two microphones on stands and a music stand on the stage, and an electric keyboard to stage right. The TVs on the patio are not even on, so that's good. It's 2:55 and I imagine he will play a couple of songs to start the event. As far as I can tell, we are the only other musicians here.

At 3:04 Fred makes some announcements about it being the start of the open mic and if you want to sign up, the list is right up front. He also says that there's an electric piano and a guitar available if anybody hasn't brought an instrument but still wants to sign up. We are the only people on the patio porch right now, except for a group of 11 other people who are together at one big table and are speaking Spanish.

I don't remember how I found this open mic, but I think it was a post on social media. When I went to the venue's website, it wasn't listed, so I called ahead to make sure it was still going. I don't know if it's too hot or if it's just not advertised very well or how long they've been doing this, but there are still no other musicians here at twenty minutes after 3:00.

Our host plays songs for half an hour and there are still no other musicians here. Rocky is tuning his guitar as the host asks him if he's ready. Rocky says almost, so Fred is going to play another song.

Rocky starts his set at 3:34. I joke with him that I think he's going to be playing a long set today; we'll see how long he goes.

When Rocky plays the song "Ghost Riders In The Sky" I wonder idly if there's an acronym hidden in the title? Ghost is G, Riders is R, In is I, The is T, Sky is S, spelling out grits like this G.R.I.T.S.

The 11-top is a big family having food and drinks and they've actually clapped a few times for Rocky, and they sing along while he plays the Elvis song "Can't Help Falling In Love." But right at the end of that song they all leave.

Despite how hot it is outside, I order some onion rings (and a cold beer). We started out by ordering a couple of unsweetened iced teas, just trying to spend a little money to support the open mic. Now there is nobody here but me and the host and Rocky is still on stage playing and it's 3:51.

It's 4:04 and Rocky is still playing when a gust of wind knocks one of the umbrellas into the microphone stand and the other umbrella, so I head to the stage area to help Fred set them up again. I talk to our waitress and ask her if there are usually more people here for the open mic and she says yeah, the patio usually has more than four people with guitars. She adds that they do this every Sunday and she doesn't know why nobody's here. I say that maybe it's just too hot, and she agrees it's a possibility. I ask her how long she's been working here and she says five years. I asked how long they've done the open mic here and she says about two years, and then there was a break during the shutdowns. Then they started right back up, so they've been doing the open mic on Sundays for a while. I tell her that I thought Paper and Strings were hosting today and she says they split time with Fred and do every other week. I make sure to tell her that we had gone to Mickey Quinn's in Seminole and that Paper and Strings told us about this one. I want her to know that they spread the word of mouth and tell people to come down.

I know that my Wednesday, Thursday and Friday gigs were slow this past week, and it was probably because the Fourth of July weekend extended into Monday, turning it into a five-day weekend for a lot of people here in Florida. They probably spent all their money on beer, cookouts, and gas for the boat, or travel and all that kind of stuff with that long weekend, so maybe people are still spent from that. Although my gig the previous afternoon and the night before were very busy.

It's 4:08 when Rocky finally stops playing and our host has turned on his pad and is playing music through the speakers. At 4:26 he turns off the music to play some more songs, so Rocky and I are going to hit the road. Not every open mic or every week will be well attended, and every venue will have a slow day. I hope the next week will be super busy for them.

CREATIVE GRAPE

THURSDAY, JULY 20TH, 2023
ST. PETERSBURG, FLORIDA

Rocky and his wife pick me up at 4:00 and we arrive at Creative Grape in St. Petersburg just before 5:00. The open mic is supposed to run from 5:30 to 9:00. We bring Sue's harp and Rocky's guitar inside. There's no host around yet, so we are looking over the menus and hang out.

Our hosts arrive and bring in a mixer. Rocky signs up on the list. We have two hosts tonight. One is named Brian and the other is named Chris, and they both seem like very nice guys. We order some food and drinks while they're setting up the PA. The place has a very cool art gallery thing going on, with a really clean and nice vibe. It's a wine bar with craft beer and they have small plates of food prepared by a Japanese chef.

By 5:30 several other people have shown up with guitars. The hosts have set up a couple of small speakers on stands and a couple of microphones. One of the hosts has a violin and what looks like an Ovation brand mandolin. The other has an acoustic guitar and a set of bongos. Business is picking up and I notice that we are surrounded by residential neighborhoods, so lots of people are probably getting off work and coming out for food and drinks.

Mark Hanson pulls into the parking lot and comes inside. Evidently, some other musicians have invited him out. Today is Rocky's birthday, and I didn't know that Brian Leneschmidt, who was interviewed in SAM 2, was born today as well. In SAM 2 we also did Chase Harvey's interview on *his* birthday, which is *also* today. That's amazing!

Our hosts begin at 6:00. One is playing acoustic guitar and the other is playing violin. They make some announcements plugging their websites and an upcoming porch music festival which is happening soon in the neighborhood.

They tell us that they are improvising an instrumental and that they always start the open mic by making something up. It sounds pretty cool. They play four songs and two of them are originals.

Rocky and Sue are the first act on the list. They have some technical difficulties at the beginning of their set; for some reason, the harp wasn't coming out of the PA, so Brian uses the second microphone on the harp and it's sounding wonderful. I think it's a pretty good mix tonight. Rocky and Sue play four songs.

The next performer of the evening is a harmonica player from Nashville who now lives in St Pete. He has some backing tracks and he's playing harmonica to that. I thought this was a different guy, but Rocky is pretty sure that we saw him at the Chill Room open mic. He is doing different songs tonight. The last time we saw him he was doing Stevie Wonder songs.

After four songs, we get a Solo Acoustic Musician we saw play a set of funny original songs at the North End Tap House. Halfway through his first song, both of our hosts join him in the stage area. One's playing the violin and the other is playing the bongos. They are good friends, so everybody's having fun with this. Then out of nowhere, something happens —the guitar lets out a big swell of feedback. Chris, the host who is playing bongos, fixes it quickly, but it startles everybody. There are forty-two people in the room, and I think about ten guitar players have signed up, including one duo and one ukulele player.

Our next act is a duo with a man on an acoustic guitar and a female singer. I step outside to sit on the porch with Mark Hanson — I think I'm finally over this whole open mic thing. I've gone to so many in such a short amount of time. I ask Rocky if he wants to leave soon and he says he wants to stick around to hear Mark play. The list is right by the front door and I glanced at it as I walked by. There are ten acts signed up and Mark's four or five spots farther down.

It's a very well-attended open mic and everybody's having a good time. I have just been to, like, 25 open mics in the last six weeks or so and I think I'm done.

Rocky and Sue come outside and we leave around 7:30. I'm just burned out on open mics. It was nice that they changed their minds and were ready to go as well.

Tonight's event was very well attended, sounded good, and the hosts were polite and nice. They even told jokes and things. The food was pretty good, and people clapped and reacted well to the musicians. I was very happy to find this little spot down in St Pete. There were several people that we had seen at other open mics, and another one of the hosts we knew was even in attendance. I will definitely come back to this spot in the future. They do hire SAMs for Friday and Saturday nights, and I think it will help me get a gig there to play at this open mic sometime soon.

RAGNAR RACE VACATION

What is a vacation?

1. An extended period of leisure and recreation, especially one spent away from home or traveling.

"He took a vacation in the south of France."

2. The action of leaving something one previously occupied.

"His marriage was the reason for the vacation of his fellowship."

I have been goofing around with creating a term for playing gigs while on vacation or using gigs to create a vacation situation. I like Gigcation or Gigacation. Several times in my life, a gig has become the anchor that paid for me to travel. Sometimes I would drive and sometimes I would fly, but a gig would cover the gas or the flight.

Sometimes I would do this so I could see friends or family who live far away, and stay with them. Sometimes my lodging would be part of the deal with a venue, included in my performance fee. I talked about this in SAM 1, in the booking chapter under the sections of the giveaway, the break-even, and the takeaway. I guess the spirit behind my idea of the Gigcation is that I am using my skills and abilities to go somewhere far away from home, to have fun and enjoy some kind of adventure.

On a trip for relaxation to Key West, I brought my guitar in hopes that I could play at an open mic one night. I was in a relationship at the time, and she did not want me to be working and playing gigs every night of the week we were going to be there. The compromise was that I still might want to noodle around on my guitar at the hotel or go to an open mic one night.

I did a little bit of research before we left and found a few options for open mic events. One on Monday, one on Tuesday, and one on Wednesday night. I could just go with the flow and stop in at whichever one of those worked for me and my ever-evolving schedule. This trip was around 2010, and I did make it out to one of the open mics. While I was there, I made a few new friends and stayed in touch with them when I got home.

Once I was back home and playing my regular gigs, I was offered a special opportunity by a local brewery that was one of the sponsors for a Ragnar Race from Miami to Key West. I was asked to provide music at the finish line, which would be at Higgs Beach in Key West, Florida.

The Ragnar Relay Series is a series of long-distance running relay races. Teams of 6-12 runners run approximately 200 miles over two days and one night. Founded in 2004, Ragnar hosts both road and trail relays across the U.S. and Canada. With 20 relays in different locations, the Ragnar Relay Series is the largest series of relays in the United States.

I believe this was two years after my Key West vacation, in 2012. I had stayed in touch with some of the musicians I had met who lived there year-round, and I reached out to one of them and asked if they wanted to join me at the gig and if I could crash at their house for a few days. It turned out to be a good idea for multiple reasons.

This guy played steel drums and electric guitar and it would be a lot of fun to have him join me on the gig. It was scheduled from 8 AM until 5 PM, an all-day job. He could handle playing some songs by himself on the steel drum and could join me with his electric guitar so we could fill time both as solo artists and as a duo. I would also DJ some music from my laptop and fill some time that way. I was able to secure $1000 for me and another $400 for my friend.

It is a long drive from Tampa Bay to Key West — it typically takes me about eight hours to get there. I got up early and started on my way, hoping to make good time. At the other end of Alligator Alley, which is the nickname for the highway that runs through the Everglades, I turned off at the first exit ramp to drive through Homestead. I take this route pretty much every time I go to the Keys because I don't like the Miami Turnpike. I like the smaller roads and the little towns along those roads that have an old Florida feel. Sometimes I even take the old road through the Everglades on Route 41. It's pretty cool to see all the airboats; maybe one day I will even take some time to go for a ride on one of them.

As I was making my way along the two-lane road, something strange happened — a bird dive-bombed at my windshield. It really was the strangest thing. The bird pulled up at the last second but still glanced off the glass and left behind some feathers, blood, and what appeared to be poop. I thought, "What a crazy bird."

A little bit down the road, the same thing happened again. This time, I saw the bird before it made its move. There was a construction zone and there were barrels all along the sides of the road making it a tight fit for the cars, but we were still moving along pretty fast, staying over fifty miles an hour. I saw a rather large bird ahead, on top of a barrel on the side of the road. It perked up its head and jumped into flight, headed straight towards my minivan.

At the time I was driving a Ford Windstar and it was a reddish-maroon color that I didn't like too much. This bird also pulled up and the last second and flew away. It almost hit my windshield on the passenger side, and I tried not to freak out as I was driving. I did, however, figure out why this was happening, and as soon as I got out of the construction zone I pulled over and stopped so that I could address the problem.

I think it was about a month before that I was in a store and bought a toy. It was just an impulse buy for fun. It was a soft plush turtle with a hard plastic shell, and a girlfriend of mine had stuck it in the passenger side "oh-shit handle." I realized that I was driving through the Florida wildlife areas and these birds were predators with keen eyesight and they were seeing this little toy turtle and going after it as a meal. So after I pulled over I walked around the van so I could take the toy down from the passenger side handle.

What is the car handle thing called?
Mueller's answer: they are called Assist Grips
from an engineering perspective, or Grab Handles
from a retail parts perspective. Colloquially, the
polite term is the panic bar. For the irreverent,
the preferred term is Jesus handle.
What's the handle in the car for?

According to Technology.org, grab handles are mainly
there so people can climb in and out of cars with ease.
If you're getting into a large vehicle, for example,
you might use the handle to hoist yourself up into
the car, and then again to lower yourself back down
onto the step or sidewalk without having to jump.

Once I was in the Keys, I stopped off in Islamorada at Robbie's Marina and restaurant for a quick snack and to stretch my legs. I always stop at Robbie's when I go to the Keys. It has become a tradition for me, and it's nice to get out of the van for a few minutes. Robbie's is located at the 77.5-mile marker and is about an hour away from my destination. If you ever get to the Florida Keys, make sure you find Robbie's and feed the tarpon. These fish are huge, about six feet long and three hundred pounds, and you can pay a dollar to feed them.

I arrived in the afternoon, the day before the Ragnar Race event, and took my friend out for a great meal at Louie's Backyard. I found Louie's on a previous trip to Key West and I have made it a place I stop every time I go. It's a beautiful restaurant in an old house on the Atlantic Ocean, away from a lot of the crowds.

While we were relaxing and catching up, my friend told me how he had taken over the calendar and was booking SAMs for daytime and sunset cruises on a small fleet of boats owned by one company. He asked me if I wanted to play a couple of gigs while I was in town, and even extend my stay a couple of days. I was totally stoked and accepted the offer.

They were three-hour cruises and paid $300, so I was happy with the deal and those gigs were a lot of fun. I made great tips on the boats, and I got to see a couple of the world-famous beautiful Key West sunsets up close on the water. I had played on other types of boats in the past, but those two gigs were my first time playing music on a catamaran.

Back to the race: the runners would start in Miami and run through the night until their team reached Higgs Beach sometime the next day. There were thousands of runners who would be arriving at different times throughout the day.

I was set up and ready to go at 8 AM which is a very early day for a Solo Acoustic Musician like me. When I arrived to load in and set up, there was a problem with the power at the gazebo. I had two fifty-foot and one twenty-five-foot extension cords in my van and the brewery had a generator behind the beer trailer. I ran my extension cords to the generator, but it was dirty energy and when I turned on my P.A. there was a bad hum and the guitars had low-frequency feedback swells.

I had to improvise, so I walked over to the restaurant that was attached to the beach. They had a covered porch dining area and there were electric outlets on the side of the building. I spoke with the manager and explained my dilemma to him. He was nice and very accommodating and allowed me to plug my extension cord into their power outlet. He asked me to give him a minute to go flip the breaker for that zone because they turned it off at night so homeless people wouldn't use the electricity while the restaurant was closed.

The electrical outlet worked and we did our thing all day. It was a long day, but it was fun and we kept our energy up. We had brought a cooler full of sandwiches, water, and sodas, and of course, we were given all the beer we wanted as well.

At one point during the race, a team from the Tampa Bay area arrived at the finish line and they were super-duper surprised to see me there. The team was comprised of runners from the run club at a venue where I played pretty regularly at the time. I had even played for a fundraiser for their club in the past. It was awesome! I had no idea that they were in the race and would be showing up.

After the gig, the brewery representatives included us in a dinner at one of the many awesome restaurants in downtown Key West. I was grateful and happy that they didn't leave us out. You never know who you are going to run into in this world, because when the taxi dropped us off at the restaurant , I knew the Solo Acoustic Musician who was performing inside. I hadn't seen him in about twenty years, and there he was in Key West. We had a big hug and were both surprised by this pleasant turn of events. We grew up at the beach in Maryland and both have been playing music for a living our whole lives.

My time in Key West had come to an end and it was time to get up early and make the long drive home. I had another interesting and scary addition to my adventure when I was on the highway outside of Miami. My speedometer just started going wackadoo and flopping from left to right like crazy. I was only two hours into an eight-hour drive and had no idea how fast I was going. I decided to keep pace with the flow of traffic and wait to find somewhere to pull off.

When I got off the road, I found a store parking lot and turned off my van. I am no expert at car repairs and had never experienced anything like this before. I waited a little bit and turned my van back on to see if the speedometer would be working normally. I was lucky and as I started driving again it was working fine. But it didn't last, and that was one of the most stressful drives that I have ever been through. It was like there was a ghost in the machine and periodically my speedometer would just go nuts. It was scary not knowing how fast I was going when I was on a highway and could feel the van moving at high speed. I did the best I could to remain calm and go with the flow of the other cars, but I can tell you that it was a very nerve-racking experience.

What an amazing and a little bit crazy trip to play music and spend time in a tropical destination. Between being attacked by birds and not knowing how fast I was going, my long drives to and from Key West were not lacking in excitement and drama. And this trip mostly came together and was made possible because I went to an open mic and made a friend when I was on vacation a couple of years before.

There were no hotel rooms available in Key West and without a place to stay, I would not have been able to do the gig or go on this adventure. Beyond the normal amount of tourists and visitors in the town of Key West, there were thousands of runners who were going to be staying in town and all the hotels were fully booked. My employer asked me to perform for this event about two weeks out and I didn't have much time to get the trip together. But I worked it out and had a blast. I was able to get some other Solo Acoustic Musician friends to cover my gigs while I was gone, and I made money on the deal.

COAST GUARD BUCCANEERS

Every now and then something extraordinary happens as a direct result of being a Solo Acoustic Musician. This story has nothing to do with the topic of the open mic, but I like to add some SAM life stories to each of these books and this volume is no different. I think this is a fun story and worth sharing with you. It was ten or eleven years ago when this happened.

For a few years, I had been playing music at a local restaurant between two and three miles from my house. It has beer and wine only and is known for its cheeseburger. The location is in an old downtown area that is small and has about five little restaurants and bars. It's an old house that was converted into a restaurant and it was owned by a U.S. Coast Guard retiree. The building is still there today but it has changed ownership and its name.

When I played there it was a military hangout, and people who were actively serving or had served in all branches of the military would hang out there. In Tampa, we have a large Air Force base south of downtown and there is a large Coast Guard base attached to the Clearwater airport as well. I was playing music in the bar once or twice a month and over time I got to know some of the regular customers. One night when I was playing, there was a group of new people who had heard about the place and wanted to be a part of the community. They were young and active Coast Guard "Coasties" who were working at the airport base. The group brought their significant others and families to the restaurant, and everyone was having fun. For some reason, I clicked with them — maybe it was because of our ages. A lot of the other regular customers who frequented the place were older or retired.

One guy in particular invited me to hang out with him and his wife, and over time we became friends. I was a member of Rotary International and I invited him to attend a meeting of my local club in hopes that he might join. Justin was a big farm boy from Iowa, and he grew up playing football. He was 6'4" and 250 pounds which is a formidable stature for sure.

One day he called me up and asked me if I had a gig for the following Sunday, and I told him that I was not scheduled anywhere. He asked me if I wanted to go to a football game at Raymond James Stadium. The Tampa Bay Buccaneers would be playing their division rivals, the New Orleans Saints. Of course, I said yes and marked it on my calendar.

He told me to meet everyone at his house and to ride along with all the family members and friends. He explained that he had been given a certain number of special passes for a sideline experience and that he and his crew would be doing a flyover during the national anthem. I thought man, this is so cool!

I drove over to his house on the day of the game; a few carloads of family and friends had gathered to carpool to the stadium. We had parking passes, tickets, and silver bracelets for special access. I had only ever been to two pro football games before and now I was going to get special treatment and see some behind-the-scenes stuff.

After we were all parked, the whole group went to a tunnel where we were greeted by security who checked out our bracelets and took us onto the sidelines. The only other people down on the field were state police, news, camera operators, and the teams with all the players and coaches. It was quite an experience to be that close to the players during their warm-ups, and those guys were *huge.*

Our quarterback at the time was Josh Freeman and the Saints quarterback was Drew Brees. It was really cool to see them throwing passes from that vantage point. At one point Justin's wife was taking my picture and I kept stepping back until I felt a hand on my back and heard a voice say, "Don't cross the yellow line, sir." I turned around and it was one of the state police officers letting me know I had backed up too far. I apologized and went back to the group.

We were all really excited to be there and were having fun. At a certain point we were told it was time to go to our seats and we were led around the end of the field toward a different tunnel. On the way we walked right past a goalpost and I stood there for a second to take a picture. It was interesting to see how the field was shaped — it was like a hump up to the middle that graded off to each side, and when I asked a security guard about it, he explained that it is made that way so that rain or water rolls off to the sides and never sits in the middle of the field. I remarked that I thought that would make it even harder for a receiver to jump up and catch a ball on the sidelines or in the corner of the end zone.

After we arrived at our seats, we all got comfortable and waited for the game to get underway. But before the game could start, we had to stand for the national anthem. Gilby Clarke, who was a guitar player for Guns N' Roses, walked onto the field as a stagehand wheeled out his amplifier. He proceeded to play an instrumental version of the national anthem and that was when Justin and his crew flew over the stadium in a C-130.

The C-130 is a really big plane and it was flanked by two other smaller jet fighters. The crowd went nuts! It was a hair-standing-on-end feeling when more than fifty thousand people cheered for our military planes flying over the stadium. Between the planes and the crowd noise, Gilby's guitar playing was drowned out, but he played on through the song.

The Lockheed C-130 Hercules is an American four-engine turboprop military transport aircraft designed and built by Lockheed (now Lockheed Martin).

At one seemingly random point during the third quarter, the officials stopped the game at the end of a play. If I remember correctly, there were eight members of the flight crew who ran out from a tunnel and into one of the end zones. They took off their helmets and waved to the crowd. Once again more than fifty thousand people erupted in cheers for our military members. It was a special moment.

I later found out that Justin and the crew had flown back to the Coast Guard base at the Clearwater airport and then were shuttled back to the stadium in SUV limousines with a state police escort through traffic. He told me that it was really cool to run out onto the field and be cheered on by all the fans.

During the game, I saw some friends and I went over and sat with them for a little bit. I told them about the before-the-game adventure I'd had on the sidelines. I had a lot of fun getting to know the family and friends who were in the Coast Guard group, and I was really thankful to Justin and his wife for inviting me and letting me tag along for the day.

I don't remember much about the game or even who won. After the game, we waited for about an hour for Justin to come to us. We were almost the last people to leave the stadium and believe it or not, that was pretty cool too, because how often do you get to be in a place like that when it is empty?

When Justin came out, he told us how he had got to go to the locker room and was given all kinds of Buccaneers gear. He had a bag full of goodies like a football signed by all the members of the team. He was given all kinds of swag, but the signed football was the crown jewel of the collection. We drove back to their house, I thanked them again, and I went home.

I had such a fun time and an awesome experience. I have told friends that story many times in the past and it all came to be because I was playing music and working the crowd. I got to know some of my regular customers in a venue, we became friends, and I ended up having a once-in-a-lifetime experience at a pro football game.

I like sharing stories like this because they are part of the lifestyle of being a Solo Acoustic Musician. I meet so many different people at my job and every now and then, something really special happens. Justin and I were friends for a few years, but we lost touch after he was stationed somewhere else. He used to scare me with his stories of what he saw swimming just off the beach I frequent all the time.

I am sure he is still flying planes over the water somewhere and helping save distressed boaters and people from the ocean. I bet he still has that autographed football. It is probably in his man cave where he watches college games on Saturdays and pro games on Sundays when he is off work as a Coast Guard Coastie.

 **AFTERWORD**

Here we are at the end of SAM 4 and I am happy to say that I had a lot of fun writing this book. In the first half, I tried to share with you my knowledge and experience from years of attending and hosting open mic events as well as some research I did on some specific topics that apply to the open mic event from the perspective of a SAM. In the second half, I tried to make my undercover adventures into stories that describe a lot of examples of and differences in open mic events. I hope you either learned something from me or the undercover missions or related to the concepts and stories or maybe all at the same time.

I encountered quite a few different instruments along the way. Here is a list of almost every single one, I think...

Baglama, violin, chromatic & diatonic harmonica, mandolin, djembe, percussion accessory items like tambourines and shakers, bongos, Celtic harp, bass guitar, accordion, ukelele, resonator/dobro guitar, twelve-string guitar, electric guitar, and of course lots of acoustic guitars.

There were also a few different effects pedals that were used...tuner, vocal harmonizer, and bass drum foot pedal.

I was surprised that I didn't see any electric keyboards or pianos at all. Then at the next-to-last open mic I visited, the host had one set up for anyone who wanted to use it. But I didn't actually hear any keyboard songs in all of my travels.

It's been interesting to experience all the different types of music and songs. I think every genre was represented as well as style. I heard songs that were fast, slow, and medium paced. I heard rock, blues, country, folk, reggae, originals and cover songs. There were lots of solo acts, duos, and even some jams.

I tried to be objective in my observations, which can be difficult because we all have our own tastes, don't we? I wasn't there to rate the abilities or skills of the musicians, and even if I did, that is a subjective point of view. I might like something that you don't like and vice versa. It can be a waste of time, so I tried to stick to being honest and truthful about what I was observing. I have to admit, it can be hard to separate myself from what I think is happening and what is really happening. There were a few times that I caught myself second-guessing something, and times when I thought it was too loud, and I wrote about that. You might have a different experience and enjoy that level of volume, and that's OK. I tried to be clear and concise about the information I was collecting, how I collected it, and what it meant to me along the way. I hope you enjoyed reading about my open mic adventures where I was "undercover." I thought it was a fun way to offer something new and different from the first three SAM books.

I went to many types of venues that all had different themes ranging from breweries, taphouses, a metaphysical shop, kava/kratom bars, a wine bar, a coffee shop, Irish pubs, and some restaurants. There were different atmospheres and ambiances. I also encountered lots of different people who were working in these venues as staff. I was very pleased that everyone I met was welcoming and attentive to the customers. Overall, it was a nice experience every night as far as customer service.

Only one of the open mics had sponsors. I think more open mic events should seek out sponsors to help them build their brand. It can definitely add to the status of the event. I did not ask the host there how the sponsors contributed to the event, but the fact that they had several sponsors still sounds and looks cool for them.

I count nineteen open mics on my list that I attended and enjoyed. I did go to three others where I didn't stay for the event. One was a liquor store with an attached bar that allowed smoking inside. They did not have food, either, which made my decision to skip the open mic even easier. Another one was a real dive with a smell that was a mix of urine cakes and cleaner. Also, there was a really drunk guy, a drunk arguing couple, and a host. That's it. There were no other people or musicians in attendance. The third one that I didn't like just felt off to me, so I left. I didn't feel bad for leaving and am not going to bad talk about those places. They just weren't a good fit for my personal taste and that is OK.

Not every open mic had all the things I wanted, but those three were not good for me at all. I did a little bit of online research on those venues, but I forced myself to go to them anyway and find out for sure in person.

There was one other open mic listing that I found online, and I called ahead because it was located at a winery that is about an hour and a half from my house. I am glad I called before I made the drive, because they had discontinued the event.

Out of all the venues that I went to I did have my favorites. I don't think any of them checked off every box on my checklist, but some did have most of the things that I wanted to find.

I met and observed many different hosts and musicians. There were all kinds of PA setups and arrangements. Some sound systems sounded better than others but all of the hosts were nice and for the most part very attentive to the musicians. When there was a feedback or equipment issue, every host handled the situation quickly and professionally. All of the musicians seemed to get along with each other and in a lot of cases there seemed to be a shared community where most of them knew each other. It was nice to see that there was a sense of camaraderie and appreciation for each other. One of the purposes of an open mic event is to have fun, and I think everyone everywhere I went was achieving that.

I almost brought my guitar and my microphone with me a few times, but I told myself not to because I wanted to stick to the mission of being an observer.

I remember when I used to host open mics and I used to tell some of my performers that if you don't want somebody to jam with you, it's really inappropriate if they do anyway, for multiple reasons. Here's an important one that I forgot to list. Someone in the audience could see you playing with someone else and assume that is your band or that is your act. They may be an owner or manager of another place that you want to get a gig at, and then they don't hire you based on a sloppy "jam" with people you have never played with before. It is something to keep in mind when you go to an open mic night and somebody wants to jam with you. Other people can assume that represents what you normally do and who you are.

What makes me think of that is the fact that a person who runs one of the open mics I visited takes video footage of people without asking them and posts it on social media. After he does it, he will tell them to go on his page where they can see the video and save it for their own use. But what he doesn't realize is that I'm not bringing my guitar because I don't want him to take a video of me, and I have a funny feeling he would do it even if I asked him not to. The fact is, if someone who does hiring somewhere sees me playing at this open mic on his equipment, it will not sound as good as what I can do with my own gear, and I will be misrepresented in a negative way.

I would like to make an additional comment about this subject. Something very similar happens when a venue requires performers to come to play songs at the open mic in order to get booked. What if you sound really good and confident on your own equipment? What if you have high-end equipment that is better than what is being provided for the open mic performers? What if the host doesn't mix the sound well, or uses way too much reverb, or doesn't make your guitar sound the way you normally make it sound for yourself?

At this point in my career, I would rather offer to play a one-hour audition in the afternoon for that owner, instead of appearing at the open mic, because I can control the sound and feel more confident that I am representing myself in the best way. I don't think I have ever actually gotten a gig anywhere by playing at an open mic. I don't think it's the best way for me to showcase my talents, so I don't use that approach. If I do choose to play an open mic, I'm either just doing it for fun or testing out new original songs.

I used to do it sometimes, but I rarely play an open mic anymore. I do like to watch, listen, clap, and spend a little money and be out networking and just being on the scene, which is nice to do. I play all the time, so it's fun to hear some other people play and listen to my friends.

I had not been to an open mic in years, and it was fun to do this "undercover" project. There are a lot of musicians where

I live, as you can tell, and I was happy that I was only recognized a few times. I met a lot of new people along the way and had lots of inspiring conversations. I know that I will visit some of these events again in the future. I do plan on bringing my guitar and playing three or four songs. I have even been putting some thought into which songs I would like to perform and making a short list to pick from.

I hope you enjoyed reading the book as much as I enjoyed writing it. Now, pick out some songs, look up some open mics, and get out there with your music. Try to network, enjoy the other SAMs' music, and share your own song choices. Make some connections, talk about the SAM lifestyle, and become a part of the local open mic music community. Take a break from the seriousness of the music business and have fun while making new friends. Don't forget to smile and clap.

If you want to give it a try, talk to a venue representative about hosting an open mic event. You can do it and it will be great! Make a plan with notes on what you want and use my checklist to see if you can get every box checked off. Then promote it and make it happen. You will make a lot of friends and get to know a lot of musicians as a host. Good luck!

 ABOUT THE AUTHOR

Michael Nichols has been a singer-songwriter and working musician for thirty years. He currently lives in the Tampa Bay area of Florida. Growing up singing in a church choir and the school chorus was a great beginning for his life in music. Though he tried several other instruments before putting his hands on a guitar, he didn't get into the drum set, piano, violin, or saxophone. Mr. Nichols started "gigging" for money when he was 14 years old and has played music in almost every situation possible. After all these years of playing out, he has developed a playbook of the dos and don'ts of being a Solo Acoustic Musician. Michael is still playing almost three hundred gigs a year and staying busy in his community. As a Paul Harris Fellow involved with Rotary International, he has donated money and time to charitable activities over the years.

# ACKNOWLEDGEMENTS

First of all, I would like to thank my friends Rocky and Sue for helping me with my undercover work. Rocky drove us to all the open mic events I attended except for one, and he met me at that one. He and sometimes Sue also played songs at every single event as well. It was very important for me to blend in and if I was just sitting there by myself, I think I might have stood out. It was awesome to hang out together and to hear the two of them play so many times. Thank you, Rocky and Sue!

I would also like to thank my friend Kevin for giving me the inspiration to approach this topic for one of my books. We were just chatting one day and somehow the open mic just happened to come up in conversation. I thought it was a great idea and appropriate for the SAM series. Thank you, Kevin!

As always, thank you to Phil for his editing expertise and to the crew at DartFrog Books for helping me cross the finish line on another book. Go Team Solo Acoustic Musician!!

You can find links and merchandise on the website.

Solo Acoustic Musician: A Practical How-To Guide

Solo Acoustic Musician 2: New Tips, Stories, and SAM Interviews

Solo Acoustic Musician 3: Booking A Gig

soloacousticmusician.com